Naikan
Psychotherapy

Naikan

Psychotherapy

Meditation

for Self-Development

David K. Reynolds

The University of Chicago Press
Chicago and London

DAVID K. REYNOLDS is director of the TōDō Institute in Los Angeles and codirector of Health Center Pacific in Hawaii. He is the author of many books, including *Morita Psychotherapy* and *The Quiet Therapies*, and coauthor with Norman Faberow of *Endangered Hope: Experiences in Psychiatric Aftercare Facilities* and *The Family Shadow: Sources of Suicide and Schizophrenia.*

THE UNIVERSITY OF CHICAGO PRESS, CHICAGO 60637
THE UNIVERSITY OF CHICAGO PRESS, LTD., LONDON

© 1983 by The University of Chicago
All rights reserved. Published 1983
Printed in the United States of America
90 89 88 87 86 85 84 83   5 4 3 2 1

Library of Congress Cataloging in Publication Data

Reynolds, David K.
  Naikan psychotherapy.

  Bibliography: p.
  Includes index.
  1. Meditation—Therapeutic use. 2. Psychotherapy—
Japan. I. Title. [DNLM: 1. Psychotherapy—Methods.
2. Self concept. WM 420 R462n]
RC489.M43R49 1983   616.89'14   82-21862
ISBN 0-226-71029-7

To Lynn
for whom quiet patience
and trust have
brought some
compensation

"Whatever else is unsure in this stinking dunghill of a world a mother's love is not. Your mother brings you into the world, carries you first in her body. What do we know about what she feels? But whatever she feels, it, at least, must be real."

James Joyce, *A Portrait of the Artist as a Young Man*

Contents

A section of photos follows p. 76.

Acknowledgments

Naikan is a therapy of gratitude and recognition of one's social debts. The debts accrued in writing this book are many.

To Yoshimoto Ishin Sensei, the founder of Naikan, to Yoshimoto Kinuko, his gracious wife and cotherapist, to his assistant, Nagashima Masahiro Sensei, to Murase Takao Sensei, who introduced me to Naikan, and to Dr. Kato Masaaki, director of Japan's National Institute of Mental Health, who encouraged my study of Naikan, I offer thanks. Naikan therapists and scholars, without exception, offered their facilities and wise counsel for this research. And Naikan clients, who allowed their private interviews to be taped and analyzed, who responded to questions touching on their personal lives, reflected well the self-giving spirit of the therapy.

Several friends and colleagues helped in questionnaire coding and various translations: Dr. and Mrs. H. Shimbo, Mr. and Mrs. T. Komatsu, H. Suzuki, T. Murase, and Y. Matsuno.

Mrs. Eleanor Kwong contributed her customary rapid and accurate typing of the manuscript drafts.

The University of Southern California School of Medicine limited my teaching responsibilities, allowing me to devote myself nearly full-time to completion of the manuscript.

Two Fulbright-Hays postdoctoral fellowships to Japan provided support for periods of research and writing on Naikan.

That I could write about Naikan therapy and its place in the Japanese cultural setting is in very small part a result of my own efforts. In countless ways I owe persons and forces recognized and unrecognized by me for this opportunity: as noted, the Naikan therapists and clients who talked with me; the founder of Naikan, Yoshimoto Ishin Sensei, who provided books and tapes and the chance to experience Naikan as client (*Naikansha*) and then as guide (*shidosha*); those who taught me the Japanese language; those who contributed to my anthropological education, to the funding of the research, to my travel to Japan, to my being fed and clothed and supported in numberless ways—all these people made this book possible. And a step further, I cannot take credit even for these thoughts that are being expressed here in words.

Acknowledgments

For those ideas that came from the literature originated with someone else's effort, and those that I had not read seemed to emerge from nowhere and bubble to the surface of my mind. As is true for all of us, I know not the origins of my thoughts at all. And the words written here were learned from parents and peers and teachers. To all these I am grateful.

Introduction

This book is about a Japanese therapy called Naikan (literally "nai"—inner, "kan"—observation) or "looking within." It is also about the way of life and view of life upon which the therapy is based. Naikan is a form of self-reflection or meditation that emphasizes how much each of us has received from others, how little we have returned to them, and how much trouble and worry we have caused our loved ones from as far back as we can recall.

Perhaps some who have read this far are already prepared to dismiss Naikan as negative, guilt-producing, self-punishing Oriental moralism, a sort of mental flagellation. To do so would be to risk missing even a glance into the wisdom of a transcendent lifeway. For Naikan offers this profound insight into human existence: that each of us, *by his or her own standards*, fails to live a life of balanced giving and receiving. We take without thought, much less with gratitude. And we offer little of ourselves to our world. Such an insight is not simply a philosophical generalization; it is built inductively from the multitude of specific, concrete events recalled during a week of Naikan reflection.

Naikan produces guilt, to be sure. But it is not the shallow, immobilizing guilt of the neurotic. Rather it is a healthy, realistic, penetrating guilt which prods to purposeful action, self-sacrifice, and the soothing awareness that despite one's own limitations others have continued to provide love and support. And the end point of the existential journey through Naikan's corridors is a gratitude that *must* express itself in service. All of this sounds very noble, yes, but the practicality of it is whether you eat dinner at the time *you* want to do so or at the time *your spouse* wants to (and whether you are genuinely pleased with that decision), whether you motion the car pulling out to come in ahead of you, whether you show up late for appointments, and the like.

Some say that Naikan, like Zen, can lead ultimately to enlightenment. Certainly both aim at some sort of demolishing of the ego. Zen does it through meditation and confrontation with the limits of rational thought. Naikan does it through recollection of how little of what we were or are deserves to be called a "self" in the first place. It becomes hard to separate out a "me" from all those surrounding, supporting others when one adopts the Naikan perspective.

Of course, only the outlines of the Naikan method can be sketched in a book such as this one. The practice of Naikan, like that of any therapy, involves the careful application of general therapeutic principles to each patient's case. Naikan, particularly, is rich in imagery, symbols, and history. Like Japanese Morita therapists, the practitioners of Naikan are a varied lot, each using the method in a unique way fitted to his or her own circumstances and way of being.

In essence, however, Naikan involves a week of intensive self-reflection which lasts, each day, from early morning until night. The *Naikansha* (client) is isolated most of that time, but he periodically reports his recalled past to a therapist who listens silently, humbly, and gratefully and then assigns the next topic for recollection. After the week of intensive (*shuchu*) Naikan the client may continue indefinitely with shorter periods of meditation on a daily basis (*bunsan* or *nichijo* Naikan).

It may be that self-examination must continue indefinitely as an ongoing check on one's daily social balance sheet. But there is a sense in which one can comfortably put behind the day's activities when one knows one's behavior has been upright during that day. And there is a corresponding need to replay in one's mind the day's events when it is likely that one has done wrong.

When this form of Japanese treatment is compared with Western therapies, several characteristics become noticeable. First, Naikan is a "safe" therapy in the sense that major social values are reinforced. The housewife who sees her husband going off for Naikan can reasonably expect a more thoughtful, grateful husband to return. Psychoanalysis offers no such promise (or limit). The Western housewife may not be so trusting of psychoanalytic therapy, for following treatment her husband might not return to stay with her at all.

The contrast between Western professionalism and Naikan humility is striking. After decades of research involvement with the subject of death, Feifel (1977) wrote: "What [dying patients] ask for most of all is confirmation of care and concern" (p. 7). As for survivors, "the greatest gift we can offer to the bereaved is to be with, not treat, them" (p. 9). From Feifel's perspective, then, those living in the shadow of death need most of all concerned companionship, not merely distanced professionalized treatment. It may well be that the confrontation with death magnifies and sharpens the awareness of issues that exist throughout the life course. Very likely the clients we see in psychotherapy are more in need of "being with" than in "being done to," more in need of sharing than receiving, more in need of telling their life stories to truly listening ears than themselves listening to our sage but perhaps uninformed advice.

Both Naikan and Morita therapies begin with the same premise: "I, the therapist, am like you, the client. We have experienced similar struggles, suffering, despair. I shall guide you as you follow a path I have explored beforehand." At this point Naikan and Moritist styles diverge somewhat. Moritists go on to teach their way of life in detail and leave to the client alone the moment by moment effort of living it out. Naikan therapists briefly explain their procedure and then settle in, during *mensetsu* interviews, to listen humbly to the client's progress. Shinshu-Buddhist-based Naikan provides a warmer "being withness" than the cooler Zen-Buddhist-based Morita therapy.

In this book I cannot write about Naikan the way I dealt with Morita therapy (Reynolds 1976). Morita therapy for all its variation and depth is best treated objectively, straightforwardly. One does this and this and this, and the result is likely to be that and that and that. Morita therapy is up front, on the table, precisely now.

But not Naikan. Naikan is bubbling feelings, the murky past, suppressed memories. It is charged with emotion; it generates emotion in rather the opposite way from Morita's method, which keeps grounding the charge of emotion in reality. Naikan taps the energy we use to hide our dark side from others and from ourselves. It turns that energy of camouflage into gratitude, repentance, and an awareness that we were loved, are loved in spite of our imperfections.

Morita therapy is cool, sometimes unbearably cool; Naikan is warm, sometimes unbearably so. If Morita is the stern, wise father, Naikan is the loving, forgiving mother.

Finally, let us be quite clear that Naikan does *not* ask the troubled client to look on the bright side of his problems. Furthermore, far from siding with the client against, say, her domineering mother-in-law or perfectionistic husband, as a Western therapist might, the Naikan guide asks the client to examine her own contribution to the *continuation* of the problem and the partner's contribution to the *solution*. To be angry at an injustice that we perceive has been done to us, it is necessary to consider ourselves worthy of better treatment than we actually received. When we see ourselves through the Naikan lens, however, we recognize that we are supported in so many ways that it is ludicrous to complain when life does not bring everything that we want in exactly the order and time in which we want it. To be dissatisfied is to feel that we deserve better. Yet, Naikan teaches, we have taken so much and returned so little. It is hard to demand pridefully what is due us while humbly bowing on hands and knees.

A recent court decision in the United States awarded a child (now grown to an adult) a sum of money from his parents because his upbringing had been faulty. One wonders what would have been the result if the judge and the son had done Naikan . . . or, earlier, if the parents themselves. . . .

1_____ Naikan at Nara

> I believe that when I am discontented with
> daily life it shows I have neglected to reflect on
> myself.
>
> K. S., ex-convict

My interest in Naikan began in 1968. At
Japan's National Institute of Mental Health, Dr. Masaaki Kato encouraged me to look at other Japanese psychotherapies in order to gain a
broader perspective on the indigenous Morita therapy that I was then
studying. A few years later Dr. Kato introduced me to a psychologist,
Murase Takao, who had experienced a week of intensive Naikan and
had supervised the Naikan of a Western client. Accompanied by
Professor Murase, I traveled to Nara to undergo a week of shuchu
Naikan in 1973. Correspondence and visits to Yoshimoto Sensei's
Center in Nara continued until 1978 when, for twenty days, I conducted mensetsu interviews of the Naikansha clients there. In other
words, for that period I became a Naikan therapist. Thus, this chapter
reflects my participant observation of Naikan from three perspectives—that of an outside researcher, a client meditator, and a practicing therapist. My practice continues alternately in the United States
and Japan.

THE NARA CENTER

The Nara Naikan Training Center (Naikan
Kenshujo) is housed in a large Jodo Shinshu temple in the historic city
of Koriyama in Nara Prefecture. A high wall shuts off the temple
grounds from the narrow street that passes in front. On entering the
gate in the wall, one sees a two-story structure and a small garden area.
Hidden behind the main building to one side is a smaller building
recently reconstructed to house the overflow of Naikansha meditators.
In the back is another, larger, garden area.

The temple itself has been totally converted into a Naikan facility
and living space. Downstairs are Yoshimoto Sensei's study, the
kitchen, bath, toilet, storage rooms, a small room where the Yoshimotos sleep, two large rooms for Naikan meditation, and a small office.

5

The last serves not only as the administrative hub of the center but also as living room and dining room for the Yoshimotos and the other therapists. One can generally find Mr. Yoshimoto sitting at the table in this small downstairs room when he is not doing mensetsu interviews. One wall of this multipurpose room is covered by banks of tape recorders, over eighty in all, for reproducing Naikan tapes. His formal study is mainly for entertaining visitors. Upstairs are three rooms of varied size, all devoted to Naikan meditation. A toilet and washbasin are located at the stairway landing.

The smaller, detached building is a long rectangle partitioned into rooms for Naikan and storage. It is quite a feat for Mr. Nagashima, Yoshimoto's assistant, to carry at one time four or five stacked food trays through pouring rain to this detached building. The broadcasting system for playing Naikan tapes during the week extends to this outer building.

The walls of the Naikan rooms at the Nara Center are adorned with photos, reproductions, and calligraphy suggesting Naikan themes. In the outer building are pictures cut from magazines—Queen Elizabeth, an angelic female child, and workers in a field. In the large room downstairs are photos of Mr. and Mrs. Yoshimoto's parents and several of their children as well as a Naikan text in calligraphy. In the large room upstairs are a picture scroll of Buddhist hell and judgment and another Naikan calligraphic exercise. Over the toilets and in the bathroom are visual reminders to continue Naikan at all times. The client is advised not to do Naikan while bathing but to bathe while doing Naikan.

The Client's Experience

The client at the Naikan Center in Nara may be referred by a psychiatrist, a school principal, local police, a neighborhood Buddhist priest, a friend or family member, a boss at work, or the client may come through a number of other channels. The information sheet put out by the center asks the client to call ahead to reserve the week of Naikan and to bring sheets, sleepwear, a wristwatch, and toilet articles. The fee is set at 20,000 yen per week (about $100) or 3,000 yen per day, but those who cannot pay need not do so. A map is provided; transportation is convenient. From the very first telephone inquiry, Yoshimoto makes it clear that the person who does not make an effort to do Naikan will be asked to return home before the week is over.

Naikansha clients begin arriving about 2 P.M. on Sunday. They are greeted and led to Yoshimoto's office–sitting room. There they register, pay, and, after a very brief interview, listen to an introductory Naikan tape. Then they are immediately escorted to their individual *byobu* screens (each separating off a small space in one corner of the room), informed of where the bath and toilet are, and left to begin Naikan. This whole process takes less than thirty minutes. This abbreviated settling-in period is unusual within the context of Japanese culture. Customarily in Japan's host-guest situations there are long initial delays and waiting periods that allow the newly arrived visitor to settle himself and prepare psychologically for whatever is to come. The emphasis here is on doing Naikan itself. Little is to be gained making oneself comfortable and relaxed after the long trainride to Nara. No need to talk about Naikan; one jumps into it and thus learns.

The sexes are segregated by room. Parents and children are widely separated, as are friends or students of about the same age, whenever possible. Conversation among Naikansha is thus minimized.

During or before dinner on that Sunday evening a tape is broadcast to provide another readily understandable model of how Naikan is to be carried out.

Mensetsu interviews begin shortly after the Naikansha starts his meditation. Ideally, interviews are conducted frequently at first, then taper off as the week progresses. Once during each day Mr. Nagashima passes from place to place assigning the times people are to take a bath. They do so at ten-minute intervals. Food trays are delivered and picked up by Mr. Nagashima. When the trays are placed in front of the byobu they are arranged carefully with chopsticks on the side toward the Naikansha. In every detail the client's convenience is thoughtfully considered. "Oshokuji doozo" ("Please take your meal") announces to each Naikansha that this food tray is waiting to be taken behind the screen. The food is highly praised by clients for its tastiness and variety. It is prepared by Mr. Yoshimoto in a small kitchen about nine feet by twelve feet. With tables and stacked food trays the kitchen is crowded when even as few as two people are in it.

Each morning at 4:45 a Naikan tape is broadcast over the intercom system. Speakers are attached to the walls in each room. These Naikan tapes are played at various times throughout the day (during meals, for example). They offer models of proper, deep Naikan; in addition, they provide examples of difficulties in recalling the past and of how such difficulties can be overcome with time and effort. They are of particular value in motivating a Naikansha when he hears someone of the same age and sex speaking about a problem similar to his own. Further encouragement comes from the *sensei* or teacher/guide during mensetsu interviews and, in some circumstances, from family members or fellow Naikansha who are invited to speak with (or write to) the meditating client.

The morning tape broadcast will continue as the clients get up at

5:00, put away their bedding, wash, and clean the center. This half-hour of physical activity in the morning is greatly appreciated by the Naikansha. Recently, as a result of the large number of clients, it became necessary to permit outside work in the gardens. Such excursions out from behind the byobu and even beyond the walls of the semi-darkened rooms are particularly prized by the young people, perhaps even to the neglect of some cleaning tasks inside the building.

NAIKAN THEMES

The mensetsu interview itself is a time of reporting or confessing what one has been reflecting upon during the intervening hour or two. An assignment is made to reflect on a particular person (mother, father, sibling, grandparent, teacher, employer, friend) or topic (lying, stealing, gambling, smoking, drinking) during a particular period of one's life (the early grammar school grades, from twenty to twenty-three, the first few years of marriage, from age forty-five until the Naikansha's mother died.) The assigned time-periods are sequential, working the same topical assignment from earliest memory up to the present in measured time-periods. Then a new topic is assigned and the process begins again. When a person is the assigned topic for meditation, the method of reporting during mensetsu is fixed. The Naikansha reports (1) what was received from that person (gifts, financial support, services, attention, love, and the like), (2) what was returned to that person (in terms of goods and services), and (3) what troubles and worries the Naikansha caused that person. In general, proper Naikan involves recalling that there was much received, little returned, and much trouble and wrongs done to others. Ideally, the client should spend 20 percent of the time on each of the first two themes and 60 percent of the time on the third.

Naikan self-reflection usually begins with consideration of the mother during the period of the Naikansha's early grammar school years. The aim is not to evaluate her performance critically, as many are prone to do. Rather, the Naikansha is to try to take the mother's perspective, to see himself as she saw him in those days. Particularly, he is to try to empathize with her efforts to show him love and her struggles to overcome the hurt and practical difficulties he caused her. This empathic attitude is to underlie his reflection on the three themes: much received, little given, and many wrongs and worries caused.

Put another way, deep Naikan is not just putting myself in another's place, but trying to imaginatively sense what I did to myself when I *was* that other person.

Although the above format of assigned persons and life periods is normally followed, some variance is allowed under certain conditions. One sort of exceptional circumstance involves a special problem for the client, perhaps the primary difficulty that caused him to undertake Naikan.

In the case of alcoholism, for example, the Naikansha may be instructed to reflect on the effects of alcohol in his daily life. He may do Naikan on how much he actually spent on drinks during a specified period (an abacus or an electronic calculator might be provided for careful calculation), what liquor did to his family relationships, how he behaved when drunk, his job performance, and so on. Similarly, a high school student may be required to focus on breaking school rules, lying, and cheating during particular school years; a delinquent on stealing; an adult criminal on the effects of his crimes for particular victims.

The therapist must structure the interview to meet the individual needs of each client. Perhaps an elderly Naikansha at first requires more limits, to keep him from rambling off into revery. Perhaps a younger Naikansha requires more frequent interviews later on in the week, as he succumbs to boredom. Under circumstances in which natural parents died or left when the Naikansha was an infant, foster parents or other nurturing relatives will be the assigned topic.

In every case the time period for reflection is specified, although it might range from as short as "this past week" to as long as "during your lifetime." Three-year periods are perhaps most common, but for students semester or trimester groupings are frequent, and for elderly persons longer periods of five or ten years are sometimes assigned. And those having initial difficulty remembering the distant past are often reassigned more recent time periods until they become accustomed to the recollection process.

The mensetsu interview that is usually described in print, in English and in Japanese (Reynolds 1980, Murase and Reynolds, n. d.) fails to display the variety of format and content observable in actual Naikan settings. The mensetsu process is not simply a mechanical recitation in stylized form.

The themes of Naikan (people, stealing, lying, drinking, and so forth) are like drill bits of varied sizes bored into the ground of memory. One works to see what seeps up around the bits as they bore deeper and deeper.

THE WORLD BEHIND THE BYOBU SCREEN

Personal space behind the byobu screen is arranged to suit the Naikansha. A flat, square cushion and a thicker round one are found by the client when he arrives. Whatever luggage is not kept is stored in the hallway or elsewhere outside of the area screened off by the byobu. As time passes the space becomes ordered in an idiosyncratic fashion. The hinged halves of the byobu form a right angle, and with the walls enclose a space about three feet square. The byobu can be opened in two different directions for mensetsu; Naikansha will become accustomed to facing in one direction when preparing for the interview and will prefer that the screen be opened from that direction. Even on the first day, when I left the screen open during an interview I was conducting, in order to ask Yoshimoto a question, the byobu was closed again on my return. Many Naikansha feel exposed when the screen is left open.

The Naikansha is isolated in the small world of the meditation space concealed behind the screen. The room is quiet but not absolutely so. Sounds of the neighborhood drift in through the windows. From a distance, trains, autos, people's voices, dogs barking, and roosters crowing can be heard (Miki 1967). From the living quarters below a telephone rings; the Naikansha hears hushed voices and the muffled indications of people moving around quietly.

For meditation the room is somewhat darkened. Behind the byobu the dim light is weaker yet, and the eyes are focused on a nearby point or closed altogether so that the visual sense is withdrawn into the personal meditative world. Under these conditions the main connection with the outside world is through the auditory sense, and, though the auditory stimuli become more prominent in the Naikansha's attention, they are softened and distorted as described above.

The isolation, in part, prevents the mind from distracting itself with surface (present) problems all the time. The memories from the social past come bubbling up. It becomes difficult to evaluate the degree of distortion in these memories. Their cumulative impact over time is great.

While thus withdrawn from everyday affairs and interactions the Naikansha is provided a carefully designed vantage point from which to reflect upon those same affairs and interactions. Moreover, a particular way of viewing them is gently thrust upon him.

NAIKAN DEPTH

There are fluctuating degrees of depth in Naikan. Perhaps I expected to find a gradual deepening and then a constancy to the emotion and insight level among clients. That expectation was not fulfilled. After a deep, tearful outpouring may come several rather superficial interviews, then a moderately moving menesetsu, then more routine ones. Or out of a string of routine mensetsu interviews suddenly emerges one with deep Naikan insight and heavy, flowing tears. The patterns seem to be infinitely variable depending on the tapes played, the specific material recalled, the client's willingness to do Naikan at a given moment, the neighboring Naikansha's progress, and other factors.

Similarly, the clients varied in ability to make Naikan-like responses during mensetsu. One young lady, anthropophobic, continued to be unable to produce the necessary utterances even by the fifth day. At one mensetsu, for example, she complained of her brother reaching into the bathroom for soap as she bathed, even though plenty of soap was outside the room on the washbasin. Such talk was clearly non-Naikan. It reflected the self-focus of the long-term neurotic. She couldn't imagine the situation through the eyes of her brother—*his* needs, what *he* gave. Rather she persisted in speaking of her own response (embarrassment) to his intrusion.

Others "played the game," but minimally, offering bare, stereotypical statements such as "Mother fixed lunch for me to take to school each day," "I did nothing for my wife in return," "I fought with my brother." For these clients, particularly, time passed very slowly.

Others do Naikan with fluctuating success. One client lied to me, confessed during the next interview that it was a lie, and was sure I had known all along his deception. Mrs. Yoshimoto believes that Hotoke-sama (the Buddha) is working on such clients.

A young lady defined as "stealing" the practice in her school days of buying books with the money her parents gave her for bus fare. She walked to and from school in order to use the money for books. Those were difficult times for her family of seven. If she had told her parents perhaps they could have used the money for something else. One gets a sense of the stretching of interpretations to come up with incidents of lying or stealing during the past. Or, the Naikan therapist asks, is this sensitivity "stretching" at all?

Yanagida (1980) reports ten common experiences associated with Naikan depth: (1) a light is seen; (2) the client's body feels buoyant, tears pour out; (3) people and nature appear to be beautiful; (4) the client becomes more levelheaded, sensible; (5) there is a feeling of joy, happiness, celebration of life; (6) the client feels more settled, develops the ability to take others' points of view; (7) there is a feeling of gratitude, closeness, and a desire to serve others; (8) the Naikansha has a sense of being changed in a fundamental way; (9) there is an increased desire to take proper care of oneself; (10) there is decreased anxiety and an increased sense of peacefulness.

Yoshimoto believes that Naikan works best with those who suffer most. The more severe the problem, the more motivated the client is to reflect deeply. People who believe they have no particular worries and who have no strong desire to know themselves in a new way are unlikely to come on their own to do Naikan. Such people have no "go-en" (essentially, no "karma") to do Naikan.

THE NAIKAN CLIENT

Who are these people who come to the Nara Center at a rate of about one hundred a month, sometimes forty in a single week, with the rate increasing year by year? Although clients come from all over Japan, the strength of Naikan lies in the Kansai area of Nara, Kyoto, and Osaka. This region, particularly Nara and Kyoto, represents traditional Japan with its deep roots in Buddhist lifeways. Yanagida estimates that only 20 percent of all Naikansha have come from east of Mount Fuji (the highly populated Tokyo–Kanto Plain area included) and 80 percent from west of that national symbol.

The registry book for the years 1955 through 1959 was examined. These years were the uneven early years of Naikan at the Nara Center. In 1955 50 Naikansha registered; in 1956 only 20; in 1957, 22; then a jump to 86 in 1958; and a decline to 53 in 1959. Comparing the registry-book data from the late fifties and from 1977 we find that the New Year's vacations and summer vacations continue to be the times in which the majority of Naikansha come to Nara. Occupational records are incomplete for the 1950s, but it appears that about the same occupational groups are represented, though proportions may differ (see table 1B). Particularly, there are fewer prison employees and more hospital employees who are Naikansha now. Of course, prisoners who undertake Naikan do so at the penal institution, not at Nara.

Comparing the figures in tables 1A and 2 we can see that the Naikansha population has increased in age. At least 20 percent of the Naikansha in the 1950s left the center before completing a week of Naikan. That figure is close to 33 percent in the 1970s. The reasons for these relatively high figures are discussed in the next chapter. Briefly, they appear to be related to the increased percentage of clients who are sent to do Naikan against their wills.

In the record book where Naikansha's names, addresses, ages, occupations, and monetary contributions are logged, there is also a rating of depth of meditation. This rating is a measure of the client's success at doing Naikan (see table 3). The ratings range from 0 (mainly for those who leave early and seem not to have devoted themselves at all to Naikan) to 10, the deepest level. In fact, during the 1966–74 period no one got a 10 rating. The ratings are assigned by Mr. Yoshimoto in consultation with his wife and Mr. Nagashima. The ratings are informal, offering little more than a rough approximation of the subjective evaluations of the consulting raters. Especially as the number of clients has increased and as Mr. Yoshimoto's health has deteriorated, his individual influence on the determination of the ratings has declined somewhat.

Increasing depth may occur with repeated reflection on the same event. For example, reflecting for the first time on a certain period, the client may recall only stealing money from the mother. In second reflection on the same period the client may admit to feeling bad about the act and vow not to do such a thing again. The third time may produce reflections upon the specific problems stealing the money caused the mother. Perhaps with reduced money for marketing she had to make extra trips to the neighborhood shops, or perhaps she had to ask for credit from a shopkeeper that week. Considering the event again, the Naikansha may recall ramifications such as throwing blame on a brother to conceal the theft. Although the Naikansha did not consider taking money from the family to be "stealing," there may be a change of attitude, a recognition of the family's efforts and his taking those efforts for granted. Even in this one instance, if the client were to repay the family for what was stolen, taking into account interest and inflation, what a debt would have been accumulated!

Takeda (table 4, personal communication) summarized the depth ratings from 1966–74. His results offer some idea of who does Naikan well at Nara. Takeda selected the three lowest and the three highest assigned rating categories for comparison. His data have been collapsed and reorganized in table 4. The deepest Naikan was accomplished by females aged 40–49 followed by females aged 30–39. For both sexes Naikan depth was maximum in the 40–49 year age group, tailing off neatly in younger and older groups. Females, in general, did deeper Naikan than males. Finally, no one aged 60 or older got a score of 8, 9, or 10 during this period. Naikan was particularly difficult for the elderly. The problems of doing deep Naikan presented by elderly clients are more fully covered in the section on Gasshoen Temple, where Naikan for the aged is a specialty.

The problems, the suffering, the wrongs committed against others may be classified into a finite number of abstract categories, but here, too, there appears a rich variety of common human difficulties—petty theft as a child, separation and divorce, lack of response to kindness from others, family objections to a boyfriend, health problems, trouble holding down a job, inability to make casual conversation. Some clients are sent formally by their employers, schools, doctors, courts. Others are coerced informally by family, friends, a priest, workmates. Some come out of curiosity, or in a religious quest to deepen or cure themselves. The range of motivation is broad.

The response to the week of Naikan is equally varied and broad. About one-third of the clients cry; some never shed a tear. Some sleep;

some lie about their past. Some remember well, others can't, still others remember and say they can't. Some exhibit a poignant willing- ness to please the therapist. Some are simply eager to leave.

Those who are sent by police, school authorities, parents, or the courts are often unmotivated. Such people may sleep during the day. In such cases, the first step is to take away their sitting pillows. If this fails, they are asked to leave, as are all who talk excessively or other- wise disturb the atmosphere. As is typical of Japanese therapy settings there is extreme lenience in enforcement of rules, particularly in the case of those who are apologetic and appear to be trying in spite of repeated failures. In other words, in most Naikan settings, although the rules appear severe and unequivocal, the enforcement of the rules is tempered by human concern and sensitivity to extenuating circumstances.

Again, the point here is simply that this therapy form, like any viable method, must have the flexibility to address the needs of an assort- ment of clients. The broad outlines of practical treatment can be sketched within a book such as this one, yet the myriad adaptations necessary to fit the range of clients cannot be detailed in a single volume.

THE CLIENT'S PACE

Day after day the mensetsu routine con- tinues. Those who wish to leave before the week is up are directed to Yoshimoto's office. He does not try to persuade them to stay. They are welcome to return should they desire to do so. If, however, there are a few minutes before a client's train leaves, he may be asked to listen to a tape in the office as he waits. The tape is a case history, an actual mensetsu recording of someone who wanted to go home but decided to stay. He persevered, and profited by his deep Naikan. Some clients have returned to their byobu for further meditation after hearing this tape. As is commonly found in many aspects of Japanese culture, there is an appreciation here of the state of readiness of a client to engage in some undertaking. Too much pushing, too much assertive direction is simply fruitless and, in the worst case, results in flight or other adverse reactions. It is best gently to provide opportunities for the client while he moves along at his own pace.

Sunday and Monday are busiest days of the week with the most Naikansha practicing. By Thursday and Friday at Nara nearly one– third have dropped out and returned home. Others have arrived during the week but not in sufficient numbers to fill the depleted ranks. During one week in June of 1978, thirty Naikansha began on Sunday; five had dropped out by Friday, and three newcomers had arrived by midweek.

In the past, with only eight or ten Naikansha during the week, the pace of Yoshimoto Sensei's day was more leisurely, although the work continued without break throughout the year. With thirty Naikansha, each interviewed for three minutes on the average, a single round of mensetsu takes an hour and a half, and then it is time to begin another round. A single therapist simply cannot handle such a large number of clients.

Certain steps had to be taken to accommodate the influx of meditators. Several years earlier a small outer building was rebuilt to increase the capacity for housing clients by about a third. An assistant with Zen Buddhist background, Mr. Nagashima, began doing mensetsu in 1976. Nagashima Sensei was a Naikansha in 1976, on two occasions, and again in 1977. For a time, he and Mrs. Yoshimoto helped to conduct mensetsu. Yet even with three therapists dividing the mensetsu interviews equally the pressure was great. Mrs. Yoshimoto did the cooking for thirty to forty people and ran the household. She was also responsible for keeping track of which interviews needed to be done by whom and when. Yoshimoto Sensei had a cerebral vascular accident with subsequent limitations on his mobility. Lifting and heavy cleaning were done by Nagashima Sensei. And all pitched in on correspondence, audio tape duplication, and other office work.

In the summer of 1978 nearly forty Naikansha could scarcely be interviewed by only three therapists. Yasuda Sensei closed down her Naikan practice in Shimizu to help out a Nara for a while. Experienced Naikansha were also permitted to conduct interviews. The attitude toward having a Naikansha interviewed by several therapists over the course of a week is quite pragmatic: better many mensetsu guides than no Naikan at all. Furthermore, there are certain advantages to sharing interview responsibilities, as Yoshimoto sees it. There is a training opportunity involved for some interviewers. In addition, certain interviewers do better with certain Naikansha, so there is a better chance of having a good fit between the two.

With as many as five or six persons doing rounds of interviewing, some organization became necessary. Mrs. Yoshimoto managed the general schedule. Each therapist was assigned a specific room or rooms within the center for his interviews. Yoshimoto Sensei made rounds of all Naikansha at least once a day. Mrs. Yoshimoto and Nagashima Sensei filled in as their other duties permitted. There were no formal meetings of therapists to exchange information, but therapists discussed informally special problems or progress encountered in their rounds. Of course, no individual knew the complete mensetsu history of any one client because the therapists rarely interviewed the same clients twice in a row. So if a sequence of meditation ended with an interview (say, the patient had completed reflection on the theme of

15

father, in three-year periods up to the present) the therapist simply asked who it was he wished to reflect upon next, who he had not yet covered; thus, the Naikansha was allowed to decide the course of Naikan after the first few days, with few suggestions from the guide. This flexibility is one of the essential features of Naikan. Basically, the guide is there only to listen; there need not be continuity. And the Naikansha is not making a self-evaluation on the basis of some set of standards proposed and refereed by the guide. Rather, the Naikansha is deciding, in terms of personal definitions, what was received, what was returned, and what troubles were caused; any failure is one of not living up to the individual's self-defined standards. The guide is no arbiter; anyone's attentive ears will do.

The usual donation for a week of Naikan in 1978 was 20,000 yen (less than $100) and in 1981 40,000 yen. The client brought his own sheets and toilet articles. The center provided three meals a day, bathing facilities, and sleeping accommodations. The cost remains less than that for a comparable hospital stay and even less than for a room in a moderately priced inn or hotel. Young Japanese therapists considering a profession in Naikan simply could not open a new Naikan facility for so little capital return on the investment in land, construction, and therapy time.

Although on previous visits to Nara I had conducted mensetsu a few times, during the month of June in 1978, for a twenty-day period, I made the rounds of interviews each morning. The Naikan Center was operating at capacity, which meant interviewing approximately sixty times each morning. Often the same Naikansha was seen two or three times a day, and, for three entering groups of Naikansha, the progress of the clients was observed over a week's period of time. I have conducted Naikan mensetsu in other facilities, but this period constituted my major experience as Naikan practitioner. Yoshimoto advises the Naikan guide to maintain a grateful, noncritical attitude while listening to the Naikansha's confession during the mensetsu. He emphasizes the importance of waiting for the insight of the client to occur spontaneously. There is no need for sharp interpretation, detailed instruction, or education in theory.

DIRECTIVE GUIDANCE

On the other hand, for all the gentle humility, there are some subtle pressures that are discreetly applied, when necessary, in the relentless pursuit of deeper Naikan.

The Naikansha who generalizes, who seems reluctant to clearly admit his culpability, may be asked, "Would you do this again? Why not?" or "Did you receive more or give more in this relationship?" or "Were you bad or good, in your opinion?" The expected replies are usually obvious. When one considers that on a typical fourth morning of Naikan at Gasshoen the mensetsu times for each client ranged from 1:35 to 6:40 with a mean of 3:25 (three minutes and twenty-five seconds), it becomes evident that there is more time for questioning and instruction than the simple three-theme format supposes. The degree of willingness to go beyond the interview itself to intervene in a client's life is illustrated by one therapist's request during mensetsu for permission to send the tape of a woman's Naikan to her husband by express mail in an effort to patch up their marriage and forestall the impending divorce.

"What were you doing Naikan on when you came to this decision (or this understanding of yourself)?" "How old were you at that time?" "What did your father do then?" "Did you apologize?" The client is forced again and again to specify, to be concrete. Specification is a technique used in many psychotherapies, both Eastern and Western, to move neurotic patients from abstraction and idealism to living in reality (Reynolds 1978). Vague, global descriptions of past suffering or past events are not acceptable.

Finally, the therapist may interpret or rephrase a client's report to bring it more closely in line with the characteristic Naikan vocabulary and phrasing. Broadcast tapes, too, have provided models for couching one's confession. This moral vocabulary (Miki 1972a) contains attributions of selfish motivations, e.g., *kimama ni* (willful), *wagamama* (selfish), *riko teki* (self-seeking), *jibun hon'i* (me first), *jibun dake* (only me), *jibun chushin* (self-centered), *jibun no guai no ii* (my own convenience); recognition of past errors, e.g., *meiwaku* (troubles caused), *warui* (bad), *ayamaru* (be mistaken); recognition of receiving much from others, e.g., *atatakai kokoro* (warm heart), *sewa* (aid), *okage* (with the help of, thanks to); and resolutions for the future, e.g., *omoiyari* (to think of others), *majime* (serious-minded), *sunao* (gentle), *doryoku* (effort), *kansha* (gratitude), *tanin no tachiba ni tatsu* (take another's point of view). Each Naikan setting has its characteristic preferred terms and phrases, but the ones from Nara are most widespread because of the broad use of Nara's published and taped materials.

The prodding and interpreting are not done randomly across Naikansha and across time. Some clients need to be allowed to tell their story before they can get on with the self-reflection. Therapists listen patiently to such persons for an interview or two. Instructions may need to be repeated several times in the first couple of days. Continued nonproductive meditation may result in warnings and, eventually, the request to return home.

Particularly when the Naikansha has had some appropriate insight and is tearful, the opportunity is ripe to provoke some statement of

17

negative self-evaluation from the past and some positive future purpose or resolution. Then the Naikansha is instructed to continue doing Naikan deeply, with all effort. As Yoshimoto Sensei points out, the mistaken impulse of a beginning therapist when confronted with a tearful, guilt-ridden Naikansha is to try to soothe the person: "It's not so bad; don't worry." But to do so only seems like kindness, he holds. The client's momentary upset signals the opportunity to deepen self-reflection, and it is the latter which will have long-term benefits for the Naikansha.

As noted elsewhere the random recollections of some older clients need shaping. Sometimes, however, what appear to be meandering thoughts wind around to an acceptable Naikan statement. However, to keep the client "on track" and to stimulate the unmotivated, resisting meditator, the therapist must exert directive effort and extend the time of the mensetsu.

Mensetsu Guides

Circumstances dictate who will do interviews at the Nara Center. On Saturday, those Naikansha who are likely to become Naikan therapists later are asked if they would like to do mensetsu of other clients. Occasionally, the invitation is extended even earlier. By Saturday they are considered ready for a training experience as a therapist. Such occupational representatives as hospital staff members (those who work in settings where Naikan is practiced), prison guards, teachers, and the like are invited to do mensetsu. They usually observe once or twice, then do the rounds while an experienced guide observes their first attempts. While observing, the person not actually conducting the interview remains out of the Naikansha's sight. As the byobu is pulled back and out, it hides the presence of an observer.

Thus, the mensetsu almost always takes on the aspect of a one-to-one confession. The Naikansha may know of an observer's presence by the sound of a second set of footsteps approaching, or the client may notice the observer as others nearby are interviewed. The presence of an observer is not a secret. It is only unrevealed during the interview so as not to distract from the intimacy of the listening relationship.

Those who come for a second week of Naikan (or longer) may be invited to do mensetsu earlier in the week. Particularly when the number of Naikansha is great and staff resources few, these experienced Naikansha will be called upon for interviewing assistance, for help in the kitchen, and for other temporary tasks.

The length of time necessary for a mensetsu varies with the interviewer, the Naikansha, whether the interview in conducted earlier or later in the week, the total number of Naikansha to be interviewed, the other tasks facing the interviewer, and so forth. During the period in which precise measurements were made of mensetsu times, the mean length for Yoshimoto's interviews was 3.5 minutes with a range of from 1.5 to 7.5 minutes. Nagashima's mensetsu ranged from about 1.5 to 5 minutes with a mean of about 2.75 minutes. My mensetsu times revealed an equally wide range but had a somewhat shorter average time.

The Mensetsu Process

At the Naikan Kenshujo the mensetsu process actually begins as the shidosha (guide or therapist) kneels and bows before the screen that bounds the physical space of the Naikansha's meditation. That time of bowing, I discovered, was very important. This silent moment helps erase the last encounter from the mind and clears one's thoughts for the next exchange. (Throughout the mensetsu both formula responses and silence facilitate deep listening. That is, when I am talking or need to formulate a response, my mind begins moving in those directions and does not fully focus on what others are saying to me—and to themselves. So stereotypical responses and silent listening allow the therapist to devote more attention to listening fully.) Then the shidosha pulls aside the screen and both participants bow to each other. A formal greeting, such as "Good morning" follows. Then comes the inquiry, "What have you been reflecting upon during this period?" The Naikansha reveals what he has received, what he has returned, and what troubles he has caused the person in question during the particular time in his life that is being considered. A new assignment is then made. "Are there any questions?" he is asked. If there are none, the shidosha thanks the meditator for his effort. They bow. The guide returns the screen to its former position, walling off the client in his own internal world. The shidosha bows once more and moves on to the next screened eddy of silence. The more mensetsu I conducted, the more I became comfortable waiting. At first, I jumped right into a pause in the interview with a direction, a question, or a closing of the mensetsu. Gradually I was able to give the Naikansha the time he or she needed.

On 6/23/78 my journal entry was as follows: "As I slide back each screen to reveal the waiting Naikansha, it is like opening a tunnel into the past. The client sits at the mouth of the tunnel, facing the present moment, but shortly he will turn back to look down the tunnel again. Some tunnels are shorter than others. Some seem to swallow up the voice, the eyes, the thoughts of the Naikansha."

Perhaps once every third visit or so Yoshimoto Sensei will ask the client if he has a question, tapering off that form of inquiry as the week proceeds. While attending the confession, the shidosha is to listen with interest, thankfully. He is to make no statement of judgment or interpretation. The process itself will direct the client to judge himself "like a prosecutor." There is *never* a direct challenge of the client's statement or interpretation of an event. The listener accepts *everything*. But sometimes a pertinent question is asked in response, requiring the client to rethink his position.

An interview can be interrupted by a telephone call, the announcement of bath-time assignments, or a visitor to the center (but it continues to the end if a tape broadcast begins unexpectedly). On returning from the intrusion the shidosha apologizes and goes on immediately from the point of the interruption, if the break has been reasonably short.

ASSESSING PROGRESS

Certain clues indicate the client's progress to the experienced *shidosha*. Does the client eat everything on the tray, cleaning the plates as though washing them? If so, he is showing gratitude and concern for the one who must wash them. Tears in males may indicate deep Naikan, but not necessarily. How much of the floor space does the byobu screen take up? How neatly are objects arranged behind the byobu? The way in which the bow of greeting is performed, whether perfunctorily or wholeheartedly, is another clue. The client's voice contains information about his progress—whether slow, soft, distant, paced with pauses and outpourings of expressions of repentance. The level of politeness of speech is useful information. Clues of posture and facial expression are read by the skilled therapist. And, of course, the content of the client's confession is important. The ability to recall and express, the degree of repetition, the apparent preparation, the detail and subtlety of the recognized dispensations and wrongs, all are data for evaluation of progress.

The stylized framework for doing mensetsu allows variations across time and individuals to stand out sharply. Similarly, small movements from an otherwise immobile therapist probably have an impact on the client's behavior. For example, at a time when the client has been crying he may perceive a shift in the therapist's position. The client may interpret such restlessness to be the result of his own insensitivity, his own excessive tearfulness which has caused the therapist discomfort. This area of unspoken communication needs further study.

At Nara, I could not detect any reinforcement of crying or self-blame through head nodding, smiling, or verbal cues. Yoshimoto Sensei sits in formal *seiza* position, legs tucked under his body, with an impassive face. He fidgets, scratches his ear, rubs his nose, but at times not obviously connected with mensetsu content, apparently in response to inner cues. When the client's tears start, the therapist's posture and facial expression don't seem to change. But whatever the emotional level of the client, the *shidosha* requires specification of details of the client's story. For example, in the midst of a tearful confession he may ask the Naikansha's age or the age of her children or some other detail relevant to the confession. On the other hand, clear verbal and nonverbal reinforcement of "appropriate" content material was observed to occur at Gasshoen Temple, another Naikan facility described in detail below.

Mr. Yoshimoto believes that most genuine meditation occurs in the first thirty minutes after the interview. So that period should be the minimal time between interviews. The maximum time permitted to elapse should be about two hours.

COMPARISON WITH PSYCHOANALYTIC FREE ASSOCIATION

Comparing the therapist's attitude in psychoanalytic free association and in Naikan, one can discern important differences despite superficial similarities. Underlying the impassive, unrevealing face in Freudian therapy is a mental process of evaluation and analysis, a rational process aimed at understanding why the patient makes such utterances. In Naikan the underlying process includes some evaluation and analysis but it carries a heavy tone of gratitude. Naikan therapists make informal comparisons of their own methods with other therapies.

In psychoanalysis the patient can project any feeling onto the therapist's blank demeanor. That is the very point of the concept "projection"—the patient's neurotic distortions of reality, learned in the past, are projected onto the blank screen of the unseen or unrevealing face of the therapist. Thus, the distortions become clear. In Naikan the therapist forthrightly offers a projected model of gratitude and commitment. "Thank you for expressing these reflections to me, please continue earnestly."

I almost wrote "*humble* gratitude" in the sentence above, but the image is somewhat more complicated than that. For all the bowing and kindness, a *Sensei* is still a *Sensei* (a revered teacher-guide). The speech forms he uses are polite and kind but they are not the forms an inferior would use with a social superior. And at the Nara Center the shidosha looks the patient in the eye as the mensetsu takes place.

ZADANKAI MEETINGS

Zadankai (literally, "sit-and-talk-meetings") are normally held on Monday and Sunday mornings each week at the Nara Center. The Monday meeting is aimed at introducing the clients to Naikan, handling any immediate questions, and motivating them to do well. The Sunday meeting wraps up the week, providing a public forum for testimonies and confessions. In addition, it offers an opportunity to encourage clients to do daily (*nichijo* or *bunsan*) Naikan after leaving the center.

The clients are called together in the large tatami-mat room upstairs. Each brings his own cushion. Because of Yoshimoto Sensei's recent stroke and consequent leg problems, he usually sits on a stool. Previously, he sat on a cushion, too, at the level of the clients. A microphone is used and the session is taped. Each zadankai may last an hour or two.

Opening Zadankai

Legitimation is a key feature of the Monday meeting. During a couple of typical opening sessions Yoshimoto emphasized the two presentations on Naikan at the International Congress of Psychosomatic Medicine held in Kyoto in 1977. He mentioned that Dr. Takemoto had sent two-thirds of his staff for Naikan, bearing the expense for travel and training himself—an investment of over three million yen. Yoshimoto had been invited to set up Naikan facilities in prisons from Hokkaido in the north to Okinawa in the south of Japan. Employees from delinquency rehabilitation facilities throughout Japan come to the center for training. A West German prison official came to the center as did an American anthropologist. These topics serve to validate the importance of Naikan in the eyes of the clients.

A second theme involves the elicitation of hope. The major technique involved here is the presentation of successful cures. For example, on one occasion the case of an elderly man from the previous week was discussed. He came not because of his illness (and had some initial difficulty doing Naikan) but by the end of the week a swelling on his thigh had completely disappeared. "If one devotes himself wholeheartedly to Naikan even such problems can be cured," Yoshimoto remarked.

Vignettes of treated cases are chosen to coincide with the known needs of the clients who are listening. Psychiatric hospital patients, suicide attempters, alcoholics, juvenile delinquents, or others may be mentioned in these selected vignettes. Experienced Naikansha—those who have been to the center before, those continuing on for more than a week, and those who began at midweek—may be asked to say a few words to the group.

A third theme is a sort of pseudoscientific structuring of Naikan. Borrowing from an already simplified explanation of brain function put forth by the well-known Ikemi Yujiro of Kyushu University, Yoshimoto points to a diagram of the brain and describes brain functions in terms of specific areas of this organ.

In general, "deeper" Naikan is equated with deeper functioning and deeper layers of the brain. Of course, the use of "deep" when referring to the manner in which one does Naikan is metaphorical. Nevertheless, there is some persuasive element added by the juxtaposition of the term in these contexts. Yoshimoto (and Takemoto) point to the relationship between tearfulness, emotion, and the hypothalamus as evidence for the parallel between depth of Naikan and layer of the brain, associating mere verbal response with external cortex. In fact, brain functioning is much more complex than it appeared to be to researchers even five or ten years ago. So, although the theoretical position explained to him is outdated (and undemonstrated in any rigorous sense), it still provides the unknowing Naikansha with a feeling of confidence in the physiological and medical underpinnings of the treatment he is about to undergo.

A fourth theme is the religious structuring of Naikan. Using visual aids depicting judgment and hell in Buddhist perspective, Yoshimoto outlines the Jodo Shinshu position on enlightenment through gratitude and service. Details of a Buddhist consideration of Naikan are presented in the section on Gasshoen Temple, another Naikan facility with a strong Jodo Shinshu identification.

A fifth theme is a general introduction to Naikan. Isn't it unusual, Yoshimoto observes, that if a stranger gives up his seat to us on a train, we Japanese thank him, but if our mother does the same thing we consider it natural, not worthy of thanks? If a stranger gives us one hundred yen we are pleased and grateful, but if our mother gives us one thousand yen it is nothing special. The reflection on mother love is a shortcut to satori. Shuchu (intensive) Naikan is like practicing a swimming kick at the side of the pool. The same formula is repeated over and over. When the skills of gratitude, appreciation, and service have been developed, such an intensive, rigid format will be unnecessary. Naikan-like thinking will permeate one's daily life.

Naikan is an economic pursuit, in a way. I'm a businessman, Yoshimoto says, and Naikan is a way of figuring out the balance sheet between the Naikansha and his mother, his father, and others. Learning to think from another's point of view will change even the smallest aspect of everyday behavior. The Naikansha who reflects deeply will eat so fastidiously that his plate will appear to have been washed when he has finished eating. The clean plates indicate his gratitude for the food and concern for the person who washes it later. Moreover, the Naikansha is on the path to becoming a Buddha. Thus we bow to him four times during each mensetsu.

Of course, the themes of these Zadankai meetings are interlocking in the sense that information, religious instruction, and scientific-sounding theory add to legitimation which, in turn, contributes to the engendering of hope.

23

Concluding Zadankai

The Sunday morning, or concluding zadankai begins about 6:40 A.M. each week. This session's audio tape is reproduced for those Naikansha who wish to purchase it. As the clients arrive for the meeting they are asked to sit near the front of the room if they intend to make a public statement for the tape. After the week-long period of isolation and silence the clients are motivated to listen and, often, to speak. The hour or two of this zadankai pass very quickly.

During the meeting, public statements in response to Yoshimoto's questioning are varied in content but relatively emotion-laden and open. One fifty-three-year-old man thought during the first day or so of the week that he had done more for his mother than she had done for him. "If so, you are such a superior person you don't need Naikan," he was told. On further consideration he realized how much he had received from his mother. This relevation was a shock with somber effect until the fifth day, when he joyfully realized how much he was loved. From that day his presenting complaint of depression cleared. Another male promised he would refrain from drinking alcohol as much as possible, but would not state that he absolutely would not drink again. A forty-one-year-old man who came because his daughter was sent to do Naikan by her school expressed his surprise at Yoshimoto's admonition to do Naikan as if he might die at any moment. He had not considered death seriously until that time. A young psychiatric hospital technician, sent by his hospital director, admitted that he came only to say he had come. At first he simply memorized his answers and invested most of his time in looking out the window. On the fourth or fifth day the Naikan theme of lies and stealing had a great impact on him. He realized that he had not been thinking of his patients as people worthy of respect. His attitude changed completely.

A middle-aged male had believed previously that he had grown up unaided by anyone. During Naikan, particularly after listening to a couple of moving tapes, he realized that he had been raised by many people, especially his mother. His words were interrupted by sobs and moments of silence as he fought to control his tears. A twenty-two-year-old woman came to discover herself. "Before, even if I didn't say anything directly to Father, I felt grumbling and anger in my heart." Yoshimoto asked her for permission to play the recordings of her mensetsu to others. She agreed. An elderly woman returned for intensive Naikan because she had had trouble doing daily Naikan after her first stay in Nara. "Before, I was grateful only when it was convenient for *me*," she said. A thirty-four-year-old woman spoke of making a tally of how much her parents had spent on her upbringing. She gave her mother a present of a week of intensive Naikan on Mother's Day.

"If you were a young man choosing a wife, would you want one who had run away from home or one who hadn't?" Yoshimoto directed this question to a young female runaway. "If your husband asks you to come back to him, in what ways will you be different?" "If he doesn't want you back what will you do?" "How has your attitude changed toward your company president?" "The Naikan of which person has the greatest impact on you?" "Who do you want to tell about Naikan?" "Has your attitude changed?"

A male in his thirties told the group that until now he had acted kindly but in his heart was not truly kind. He planned to come back to Nara for more Naikan. A seventeen-year-old high school student reported that his drinking problem was cured but not his smoking. A fifty-two-year old man gave up smoking, and had three packs of cigarettes untouched in his bags. A thirty-one-year-old male came to the center for the first time after listening to a Naikan tape of the person now sitting, quite by chance, next to him. Both had returned for subsequent intensive Naikan. A company head read a poem about "Mother" and cried.

The Sunday zadankai gives Yoshimoto the opportunity to press for daily Naikan after the clients return home. As described elsewhere, daily Naikan, or nichijo Naikan, is done twice daily. For an hour in the morning one reflects on the persons in one's past in ordered sequence just as during intensive Naikan. In the evening one reflects on the persons encountered during that day—what was received from them, returned to them, and the troubles caused them through one's mistreatment, lies, and so forth.

Yoshimoto emphasizes that with the week of intensive Naikan undergone at the center the clients' self-reflection has just begun. Naikan must become a daily habit until it permeates attitude and behavior. Clients are asked publicly if they will do Naikan daily. Most often they give a vague, rather noncommittal reply. Those who promise to do an hour or more each day are praised and put forward as examples to the others. Yoshimoto commonly cites the lady who has been doing daily Naikan for eighteen years. Faithfully, each week, she sends a postcard describing the highlights of her meditations.

Technique

Certain elements of Yoshimoto's style in conducting these zadankai meetings are worthy of discussion. The first element to be considered here will be handled more fully in a later chapter; it is the use of concreteness and specification. When Yoshimoto describes his own history, one of turning from the life of a businessman to developing Naikan, he offers specific dates and concrete instances. Back in 1956, for example, he visited such-and-such a prison to lecture about Naikan. At that time the warden there was so-and-so. Similarly, when he cites case histories of successful Naikan-sha, he gives from memory their names, occupations, ages, and the months and years (and sometimes the days of the month) in which they did Naikan. Yoshimoto expects the same sort of concreteness when Naikansha speak publicly at the zadankai. Vague, general statements are not permitted. The kind of ideal response is illustrated by a middle-aged lady who was asked whether her attitude had changed while doing meditation. "Completely," she replied, "For example . . . ." And she went on to specify how this change was manifested.

Yoshimoto often forces black-or-white answers. One female, during mensetsu, was made to choose whether she had been a good or a bad wife. Will you do daily Naikan? Have you determined to give up drinking completely? Yes or no, Yoshimoto asks. Kondo (personal communication) suggests that Yoshimoto, not living in the everyday world that most of us inhabit, does not perceive the "grays" of daily existence. Perhaps, in addition, the world of religion requires absolute choices in life. The world of science deals in shifting probabilities. There is undoubtedly some comfort in the certainty of Yoshimoto's absolutism, whether or not, or to what degree, it is based on reality.

A third element is Yoshimoto's use of simple stories and illustrations selected to meet the particular needs of the clients. Visual aids—diagrams, reproductions of paintings, calligraphy—illustrate certain points. One analogy, for example, compares intensive Naikan with power poles and daily self-reflection with the lines between the poles. To set up poles without stringing lines between them is senseless. Not only are analogies and stories (taken from myths or case histories) easily understood, they bear a quality of believability or "proof" to most listeners (Reynolds 1976).

Finally, the zadankai confessions and tears are lightened by the sparkle of Yoshimoto's humor. People were rustling and whispering as one girl spoke of her changed life. "Please be still," Yoshimoto smiled, "this high school student is doing her homework." Again, after a man with a swelling on his rump remarked that it had disappeared during Naikan, Yoshimoto grinned and asked the listeners not to send all their friends with lumps on their tails to Nara to be cured. When asked how he handled his children's lies and stealing when they were growing up, Yoshimoto with a twinkle in his eye replied that he had produced seven children in rapid succession and left the child-rearing to his wife. He said he had to spend all his time earning money to feed so many of them.

Following this final meeting, people assemble their luggage and prepare to leave. Those who want the tape of the meeting must wait an hour or more while it is being reproduced. Books and tapes may be bought at this time. This post-zadankai period is ignored by Japanese scholars and therapists writing about Naikan, but it has some very important functions.

The spirit is light during this post-meeting period. Conversation among Naikansha flourishes. There is a shared feeling of something accomplished. Addresses are exchanged. People arrange to walk together to the train station and ride partway home together. Those with families picking them up in a car may offer a ride to a newfound friend. Similarly, the relationship between therapist and client lightens. Laughter is common. The client realizes his acceptance by therapists and fellow clients in this new transitional context. The therapist becomes a bookseller, a clerk in an audio tape store, a comrade. Then come the final bows of departure, the formal expressions of mutual thanks, and farewell.

Naikan Tapes

Audio tape recordings are used in various ways and played at different times in the Naikan facilities around Japan. Often, they are played during eating and working periods as at the Naikan center in Nara. But at every step of the treatment process, from motivating the potential client to supporting the client after his week of intensive self-reflection, the tapes are used purposefully. Because the Nara Center has the highest reputation, the largest tape collection, and the best equipment for producing and reproducing tapes, nearly every Naikan therapist uses tapes given by or bought from Yoshimoto. Sixty-minute, ninety-minute, and 120-minute tapes are available to the layman at a nominal price. They may be purchased on the Sunday morning that ends the week of Naikan, or the sale may be handled by mail.

The following transcription of the tape of a child's Naikan experience is customarily played as part of the introduction to Naikan for first-time clients. During the week of intensive Naikan the tapes are selected to meet the particular needs of the meditating clients. However, this model tape has been heard by nearly all those who have come to the Nara Center. Although the Naikansha in the tape is younger than those typically recorded, the tone and format of the tape are not extraordinary. The speakers are alternately Yoshimoto and his granddaughter.

It is 8 A.M. January 4, 1968, at the Nara Naikan Training Center. How old are you?
I'm seven.
What grade in grammar school are you?
I'm a first grader.

We're going to tape this for awhile. Let's consider your mother from the time you were three. You started in kindergarten then, right?

That's right.

When you were three what did your mother do for you? Then what did you do for your mother? And what troubles did you cause her? Please think about these things. Do you understand?

Yes.

Well, you have an hour. Please do your best.

All right.

Do you have any questions?

Ummmm. No.

No? Please do your best.

. . . .

Only thirty minutes have passed. Perhaps you have remembered something. Thinking about your mother when you were three years old, how did it go?

Well, when I was three, the very earliest time, my mother took me to school. Then, when she was leaving, I ran after her. That caused her problems.

What did you do for her?

I don't know.

What troubles did you cause her? (Pause.) Did you hit your little brother or cause troubles like that?

No.

Nothing?

No.

Please consider it some more. Next, when you were four what happened in relation to your mother? Take your time and check carefully. I'll come again.

. . . .

This time what age were you doing me the favor of considering?

When I was four.

About your mother.

Yes. When I was four Mother came to kindergarten and took my photograph. And she got my things ready for school.

What did you do for your mother?

I only rubbed her shoulders.

What troubles?

Ummm. I don't know.

Please spend more time and effort in checking whether or not you caused troubles. Next time when I come please answer this way: "I was investigating myself at age five in relation to my mother. Mother did such and such for me. I only did thus and so for her. As for troubles, I did such and such."

All right.

. . . .

This past thirty minutes what have you been examining?

My mother did this for me: She fixed my meals and made my bed for me. What I did for her: I only swept out the store downstairs. As for troubles, when I was reading a book Mother called me to help her for a minute. But I was reading and wouldn't go, so I caused her trouble.

That was when you were five, wasn't it?

Yes.

Do you think you are doing Naikan well, are you doing it better than before? Can you do it?

I can do it.

What made you want to do Naikan?

My grandfather.

(Chuckles.) Your grandfather. Did someone tell you to do it or did you have some reason for trying it?

I heard a tape.

That's what prompted you to do Naikan?

Yes.

You are doing just fine. Your parents and your grandfather are very pleased. Please continue exploring yourself in relation to your mother. What you received, what you returned, what troubles you caused. Let's continue checking.

All right.

Please continue.

. . . .

What have you been considering?

On my birthday Mother bought me a French doll, and she took my picture during our school sports meet. I took care of my little brother. As for troubles I caused Mother, I ate the hamburger that my little brother wanted, then I left some, and I ate all of the pickles.

That was when you were six?

Yes.

Next you entered grammar school in April, didn't you? Let's examine the months of April and May. What Mother did for you, what troubles you caused her. Next time I come please say, "I examined myself in relation to my mother during the months of April and May, the beginning of grammar school."

All right.

. . . .

What have you been remembering for me?

29

When I started in the new school Mother came with me. The other mothers came, too, but Mother stayed until the very last that day. And going home Mother carried some of my things for me. What I did for her . . . absolutely nothing.
What trouble did you cause her?
Trouble . . . ummm . . . Well, she bought me a treat.
Well, next time is June and July.
Yes.
Please reflect about your mother. Do your very best.
All right.

. . . . .

Now it is six in the evening. You've been doing Naikan for about ten hours. You've been doing it very diligently. Do you feel like continuing or stopping?
I feel like continuing.
Any time that you want to stop please tell me.
What have you been reflecting on?
My father took me shopping. (She begins to cry.) I didn't do anything for him.
Troubles?
I couldn't think of anything there, but he came to our school sports meet for me. (She is sniffling back tears.)

At this point the girl decided to stop doing Naikan. She couldn't verbalize her reasons for stopping when asked, but no pressure was applied to keep her doing Naikan. She was invited to return whenever she wanted to do so. Yoshimoto reports that perhaps she felt sad when comparing how much her father had done for her in comparison to how little she had done for him. The discomfort prompted her to remove herself from the setting.

Below are listed the categories of tapes used in most brochures and books where the tapes are advertised as well as the approximate number of tapes and some examples of titles in each category.

Family (31 tapes): The Elderly; Father; The Joy of Parents; Parents and Children; Husband and Wife; Love; Love Triangles; Separation; Divorce.

Work (22 tapes): About Work; A Manager; A Store Owner; A Bar Hostess; Labor Problems, *Kohai* (junior employees). This category includes lectures given at banks, manufacturing facilities, company meeting halls, and the like.

Psychotherapy (46 tapes): Cure of a Phobia; A Compulsive Woman; Hysteria; Psychosomatic Cures; Depression; Writers Cramp—Three Cases; Blushing Phobia, Hypnosis, and Naikan; Parkinsonism; Intestinal Problems and Naikan; Story of an Attempted Suicide; Body Odor Phobia; Two Men Cured of Hernia (!); Feelings of Inferiority (subtitle:

Five Suicide Attempts in Three Years); Naikan and Medicine; Lecture at Jikei Medical University; Lecture at Okayama University.

Schools (17 tapes): Grammar School; Junior High School; High School; Teachers and Naikan; Nursing School; Love between Student and Teacher; Pre-University Students.

Alcoholism (14 tapes): Stopped Drinking; Hospitalized Alcoholics; A Grammar-School Teacher's Confession; A Woman Drinker; Troubles of a Woman Married to an Alcoholic.

Penal Institutions (7 tapes): Kyoto Prison Lectures; Horses, Gambling, and Stealing; Sapporo Prison Lectures. (One private tape list includes lectures at more than thirty-five prisons and detention facilities throughout Japan).

Miscellaneous (25 tapes): Yoshimoto Sensei's Broadcasts; Zen and Naikan; Christianity and Naikan; Theory of Naikan.

These tapes well reflect the scope of interest and optimism of the founder of Naikan. Most often they include recordings of a succession of actual mensetsu interviews and discussion of the client's progress and results. They are widely transcribed and printed in Naikan-related books, magazines, and pamphlets. But they make their strongest impact by being heard—the tears, the remorse, the emotional depth of Naikan are conveyed powerfully through this auditory medium.

One problem with the tapes is that people who are not good with words, people who do not cry, and people who do not recall dramatic material cannot follow precisely the models found in the tapes. During one three-week period in Nara at least five Naikansha asked for reassurance on this point. "Is what I am doing Naikan? I feel my self-reflection is shallow compared to the Naikan of the tapes."

RAKUGAKI GRAFFITI

At the Nara Center, on wooden floors, paper screens, sliding doors and walls of certain rooms, are the carvings and scrawled messages of scores of Naikansha. These graffiti reflect the non-Naikan thoughts of the young men who carved them. Similar *rakugaki* have begun to appear at Ikeda's Naikan facility in Meguro, Tokyo. There, too, they are found only in the rooms used by males.

All of the decipherable graffiti at the Nara Center were copied and grouped into categories. One should not try to make too much of these data. They are not exhaustive representations of stray thoughts in this setting. However, they do represent some of the preoccupations of this group of Naikansha—mostly persons who have been forced to do Naikan to avoid being expelled from high school. Such clients are poorly motivated; they do shallow Naikan. The fact that they have

31

marred another person's property is evidence that they have not learned the lessons of Naikan. Yet their thoughts made visible probably are not far removed from those of other Naikansha. The reader might like to pause here and try to predict what sorts of graffiti appear in this Naikan temple setting. He or she can then proceed for some possible surprises, and confirmations.

The most common references are to time. Calendars, the number of days left in the week, the date, slash counts of the number of mensetsu interviews, the current time, and such desires as "I hope the time passes quickly" and "I hope the end comes soon." Such obsession with time runs counter to the stereotype of Japanese as infinitely patient. Naikan is a difficult discipline for nearly everyone who undertakes it. The passage of time, punctuated by mensetsu and meals, intrudes on the meditator's reflection on the past. Watches are prominently positioned within the confines of the byobu screens.

The second most frequent category of graffiti is names, particularly women's names. It is easy to imagine that fantasies of girl friends fill some of the waking hours of these young Naikansha.

Pleasures, particularly those restricted by the Naikan environment, take on added value. References to food are common. "My stomach is full." "The Itamochi Senbei [crackers] were delicious." "Seven Stars [cigarettes] 150 [costs 150 yen]." Vocalists' names appear. Sexual pleasure is represented in many graffiti. "I like king-size and will marry." "[A phone number of] someone who gives head." "Kiss plus sex." "Miss Eros." Phallic drawings and sketches representing sexual intercourse adorn even the reproductions of Buddhist paintings on the byobu screens.

Several graffiti have to do with love. "I love you." "I love you, Oki [a girl's name]." "I won't love me tonight." "I love [a car license plate number]." In all likelihood these sorts of rakugaki represent romantic love and affection rather than the self-sacrificing love emphasized in Naikan.

Complaints and thoughts about going home constitute another category of writings. "Completely boring." "This kind of crap is unbelievable." "Naikan in the morning is suffering." "Going home." "Good-bye." "So long." "I want to leave soon." Again, the stereotypical image of the Japanese as ever-enduring, passively accepting of any difficulty, becomes tarnished by the corrosion of reality.

There are a few references to darkness: "The Black Emperor" and "Nights" are typical examples. The space behind the byobu screen is dark. Most Naikansha meditate with eyes shut. Perhaps the symbols refer to the dark past or black sin. The referents are too few to allow further speculation.

A number of graffiti symbolize an organizing or preparatory function. They were written to calculate or remind the Naikansha of something he would say during a subsequent interview. Arithmetic calculations are included here (perhaps of amounts spent on alcohol or cigarettes). There are ordered sequences such as ages—"22–24, 25–27, 28–30 . . . ," the Naikan interview order for what was received, returned, and troubles caused (actually, the order was confused in one such graffiti reminder),—and the school sequence of "grammar school, junior high, high school, college."

There are notes of encouragement to self and to others. Such notes often appear to be intended for those who later would follow the same course in the same space. "Tough it out." "You who sit here for a week, stick it out." "Let the fellow who wants to, go home; I'll carry it through to the end!" "I understand well the magnificence of Naikan."

Finally, there is a category of graffiti reflecting Buddhist, Naikan, and existential issues. "Lotus." "Bissha Monten [one of the Buddha's names]." "Heaven." "Devil." "Death." "Mother." "Why?" "Self-reflection." "I am lived [a Naikan phrase meaning 'my life began and continues thanks to the efforts of others']."

A range of topics is found in these graffiti. From the fundamental self-focused references concerning food and sex to the practical preparations and mnemonics for the next interview to the existential, philosophical issues of "Death" and "Why?" This variety is important when evaluating the sorts of people who wrote the graffiti and how representative it is of other Naikansha's thoughts. But, as in many human enterprises, despite the variety, the topics can be ordered; they are not random. Thoughts worth the effort of writing or carving in this setting are of certain sorts. And what is missing is of equal interest. There are references to bosses, singers, girl friends and mothers, but not to fathers. There are references to hunger, sex, and love, but not to anger.

A final example of rakugaki from Nara:

> You don't live by yourself,
> You are lived by others.
> Everything in Heaven and Earth is lived.
> God and Buddha, too, are caused to be lived.

To understand this graffiti fully requires Naikan perspective. It is *satori*.

NAIKAN DRAMA

There is an atmosphere of drama during the week of shuchu Naikan, particularly at Nara. The stylized maneuvers of greeting, confessing, closing the byobu, and movement to the next character are reminiscent of a Noh play. The tape recorder and use of the microphone add symbolic importance to the acts. The scenes are worthy of preservation. The auditory sense is used effectively to heighten dramatic effect. The usual silence is punctuated by tape broadcasts that include uncontrolled crying and dubbed-in organ music, thus offering strong emotional contrast. The client stages his performance during mensetsu for the therapist.

This description of the dramatic element in Naikan is not meant to brand it as artificial or superficial. The emotions evoked are almost always genuine and the results profound. Rather, the point is that this manipulation of dramatic ambience has strong impact on affect and is a tool used effectively, often without awareness, to aid in the achievement of therapeutic goals.

2 ——————— Naikan Variations

> I wish to thank everything I see and feel.
> T. K., Nara Juvenile Prison

Unlike some indigenous therapies in Japan, Naikan was allowed to branch out in several directions without a strict effort to maintain a "pure" original format for the method. After all, according to Yoshimoto, his own therapeutic style developed as a variation of Jodo Shinshu's *mishirabe*.

Mishirabe is a practice engaged in by priests and devoted lay persons in one subsect of Jodo Shinshu Buddhism. Without food and water and usually without sleep the devotees isolate themselves and reflect on their past as a means of achieving enlightenment. After initial failure, in 1937 Yoshimoto himself achieved satori through mishirabe in a cave not far from the Nara Center. Easing the physical hardships and formalizing the mensetsu structure, Yoshimoto developed Naikan. How could he be concerned with preserving the purity of what was already variant?

In the pages that follow, eleven Naikan facilities are examined in some detail and a number of additional specializations, variants, and uses of Naikan in conjunction with other therapies are treated more briefly. These Naikan variations illustrate the flexibility of the method, its adaptability to a range of patient types and therapeutic philosophies and physical facilities. Further details on seven of these settings, gained through questionnaire responses, are reported in Chapter 3.

GASSHOEN TEMPLE—
RELIGION AND HEALTH

The minitruck flung itself along the narrow Japanese roads while the driver directed a steady stream of information toward me about Gasshoen, the place we were about to visit. His spoken Japanese was very fast and filled with Buddhist terms that were quite unfamiliar to me. Now and again he would draw a character or two in the air with his finger while explaining its meaning in a Buddhist context. He was a small, wiry fellow with close-cropped hair and a spotty dark tan indicating that he spent a lot of time working outside. But his most outstanding characteristic, one he shared with everyone I met at Gasshoen, was an exuberance that held back nothing in his speech, in his gestures, even in the way he worked the brake and accelerator of his truck. Such energy in the humid heat of a summer's day in Mie Prefecture, midway between Nara and Nagoya, was impressive.

We turned off the highway onto a narrow road that led to an even narrower one that stopped abruptly partway up a short cul-de-sac valley. As I looked about me, I realized that Gasshoen is not a single temple structure, as I had expected, but a complex of buildings. These buildings house a community of monks, nuns, and lay people, some permanently, some temporarily for a retreat or working party.

As I climbed out of the truck, men and women from the permanent core of members stopped their work to fold their hands together and bow a polite greeting. To my left was a temple, which consisted of a single large room, dark and cool inside. To my right was a landscaped hill with steps leading to a small temple-shrine that was also the office of the community. Behind and to the right were several buildings built like stepping stones up the hillside—a dining hall, living quarters, and a building for Naikan introspection. Above them was a long structure about half-completed. Construction workers clambored about laying the roof on what would become the new Naikan facility. Between and beyond the buildings were gardens of flowers, fruits, and vegetables of many kinds, including squash, radishes, cucumbers, cabbages, and potatoes.

I was led up the steps and seated in the shrine office overlooking the valley. The three people who would be my guides during the afternoon introduced themselves, apologizing that the head of Gasshoen, the priest Mizuno, was nearly always away speaking somewhere and rarely had a chance to come back to his home at Gasshoen during the day. The trio of persons sitting around the low table with me formed a fantastic assemblage. The second-in-charge was a nun. Tiny, and spry at fifty-four, she had a shaved head and a childlike face. A hunchback with pixie face and a wide smile, a painter of professional caliber, was my second guide. The third was an old fellow, a former farmer with stubble on his face and on his skull. He moved briskly up and down the steps and hillsides but drifted into sleep when we sat around the table talking.

They served melons and bananas as we talked in the shrine. A tape recorder was going, so all would be passed on to the head priest when he returned. I signed a guest register. The three of them laughed gleefully as I explained the name and title written in English on my name card. Clearly, I was as unique a visitor to them as their place was to me, with all my experience in Japan.

Such was my first visit to Gasshoen. "Gassho" in Japanese means "to clasp one's hands and bow." To gassho is to greet, to thank, to pray. "En" means garden. Thus, Gasshoen, "The Garden of the Bow." The next year I returned for a five-day visit, sleeping in a tiny room hidden in the back of the large temple. By then the new Naikan building had been completed, but the people had not changed. They remain joyfully devoted to their way of life.

A new group of Naikansha begins meditation on the second, twelfth, and twenty-second of each month (except in August, when special summer programs for youth take precedence). In 1976, at the time of my first visit to Gasshoen, there were some nineteen people meditating in Naikan, sixteen others living on the grounds as staff, and sixty or more townspeople living nearby who contributed regularly to the temple complex. The Naikansha who come to this facility are likely to be elderly farm women (mean age early fifties), strong believers in Jodo Shinshu Buddhism. They come with physical complaints, daughter-in-law and other family problems, and the desire to become better Buddhists.

The basic position of the Gasshoen staff toward physical illness is that it can be the means to cure the spirit or psyche even though the illness itself is not cured. Nevertheless, some attention is given to selling home remedies and health foods. Particularly *genmai* (unpolished rice) is highly touted.

Two meals are eaten each day in the dining hall. They consist of genmai and various vegetables and fruits, no meat. In the early morning only a cup of tea with a single pickled plum in it is taken.

The day begins for Naikansha at 4:45 A.M. when the sound of the temple bell reverberates through the little valley. At 5:00 all are seated for morning worship. Singing, chants, and recitations of Namu Amidha Butsu are followed by a one-and-a-half hour lecture by Mizuno Sensei, the chief priest. Mizuno is seventy-seven and full of vitality. He is an excellent speaker, much in demand. He uses short illustrations, shifts from humorous to serious topics, has a wide voice range. The content of his lectures is reminiscent of Sunday morning Christian sermons. Death frees us from too much suffering and loneliness in old age, he reminds us. The locust sheds his skin and flies off a new creature. The lecture ends with a period of questions and answers.

After drinking tea, the Naikansha set up their byobu screens and retreat behind them for meditation. The new Naikan building at Gasshoen contains a single long room for Naikan, a bathroom, and storage facilities. The byobu are lined up in two rows along the walls with a wide aisle between them. The Naikansha is concealed from his neighbors on both sides and across the aisle, but as one walks along the central passage one can easily see the meditator through the space between the byobu. Naikan meditation at Gasshoen is called "hoza," "jewel sitting." Unlike at Nara, personal luggage is stored outside of the byobu space to avoid distraction. Friends and relatives are seated far apart so they will not talk. The three elements of Naikan (what is received, what is returned, and the trouble caused) are written on a small sheet of paper for each Naikansha.

The day is broken up by the meditation periods and by two meals, three half-hour broadcasts of Naikan tapes, a thirty-minute work period in the garden, an evening worship period, a bath, and six mensetsu. For those with physical problems, particularly older women with leg and hip pains, "special" Naikan is conducted in the older building. There the Naikansha has more space and can lie down.

Naikansha are discouraged from speaking except to staff. Even at meals (taken collectively) they are to gassho instead of expressing thanks verbally when food is passed to them. In like manner, morning greetings should be gassho. Meals are preceded and followed by recitation of a written prayer.

Mensetsu interviews at Gasshoen have a unique flavor. The therapists are nuns. Their manner of conducting the interviews is efficient, extremely polite, and humble. They radiate gratitude and concern. Unlike the therapists at the Nara Naikan Center, the nuns look down as they kneel on the tatami mat and listen to the Naikansha's confession. They offer a great deal of verbal support and reinforcement. "Yes, yes." "Thank you." "That's right." "I see." "Fine." "That's important." Such responsive words and phrases frequently punctuate the confession. There is also a great deal of rephrasing, repeating, and reinterpreting the client's words. Gentle prodding occurs through questions such as: "What will you do from now on?" "How will you act toward her?" "What would you like to become in your life?"

Structuring the mensetsu is particularly needed for the predominantly elderly farm folk, whose thoughts tend to drift and ramble from topic to topic. The mensetsu guide slides neatly into the rambling confession with "Yes, yes" and repetitions of the client's own words, then she moves back to the formal structure of what was received, returned, and what troubles were caused. Or, the first of the three ordered questions is asked, "What did you receive from ———?" and, after a brief reply, the next question is asked rapidly allowing no opportunity for rambling. Time is taken during mensetsu exchanges to educate, to explain, to reassure, to listen to questions about family problems or religious issues. One grandmother was told that her granddaughter was working hard at doing deep Naikan and that the therapist knew the grandmother would want to reflect deeply also. Advice is offered. For example, a young wife was advised to respond to her mother-in-law with praise and verbal recognition of the older lady's hard work rather than with grumbling and complaints. Not only will their relationship warm up, it will be a good example for the children, the nun explained.

For elderly people larger periods of their lives may be assigned for reflection. Rather than the usual three-year segments, five-year or even fifteen-year periods are sometimes covered. Physical complaints are dealt with by requests for specification (Exactly where does it hurt? When? When did it start?), and by expressions of sympathy and advice. One woman was advised to sit erect for fifteen minutes and to put her hand over the spot on her head that hurt whenever a headache began. For those who forget their meditation assignment a reminder may be written by a therapist or by the Naikansha. For some of the elderly farming clientele there seems to be somewhat less emphasis on the mother-Naikansha relationship and more on the relationship between mother-in-law and daughter-in-law.

A remarkably low dropout rate (less than five in 1,500 over four years) appears to be the result of the strong supportive orientation, the use of positive verbal reinforcement during mensetsu, the varied program that reduces boredom, the flexible time periods assigned for reflection, and the type of person who does Naikan at Gasshoen.

Life at Gasshoen is laced with humor and laughter. The serious, sometimes tearful, side of self-reflection is balanced by joking and camaraderie. For example, during one of the post-Naikan zadankai meetings one speaker mentioned that during the previous night's lecture the priest said that the spiritually deep person listens rather than talks. The speaker admitted to being a talker, now he would like to sit down without making a speech, but then everyone *expects* him to make a speech, so he's stuck, not knowing whether to speak or not. He laughed at his predicament. Next Mizuno Sensei was called upon but jokingly said he would rather not speak and sent up another person to lecture for him. Again, laughter followed. The substitute lecturer picked up on the theme and smiled modestly, "Unaccustomed as I am to public speaking . . . ." And so on.

The content of the lectures and counseling sessions at Gasshoen reflects basic human problems raised within a religious framework. How is it best to live? How should I view myself? Why do I act as I do? Such questions need not necessarily be religious ones but they may be such.

The staff emphasizes that Jodo Shinshu is for life now, not life after death. The criticizing heart is hell now. The selfish person is a devil. One need not look to a magical afterlife. Each day we are reborn to new experiences and roles. Humans take God's or Hotokesama's heart within them by having proper attitudes and doing good deeds. The staff at Gasshoen insists that Naikansha consider why it is that they systematically forget all sorts of major and minor acts of courtesy, kindness, and self-sacrifice which they have received from others. Why is it that humans, knowing all that they do, continue to fight within families, among nations?

Naikan, they say, deals with the unseen world of the heart, the part each of us usually keeps concealed from others. Reflection should be carried out not only on what the Naikansha did or did not do, but also on the attitudes and intentions that apparently did not emerge as behavior. Stealing is not simply taking objects without permission; stealing incorporates improper use of time at work, taking minutes from an acquaintance by being late for an appointment, using one's parents' possessions without permission, returning a borrowed object late. Similarly, listening without gratitude and full attention is stealing a speaker's words.

Naikan is not merely a method of determining how evil each person is, they argue. It is not simply a focus on more and more details dredged up from the past. It involves a change of heart, a new view of self and others, and a rebirth into a new kind of life with cleansed attitudes of apology, gratitude, humility.

"Have my sins up to now been erased?" asks a thin, gray-haired lady in a faded print dress. "Certainly," she is reassured, "if you've truly repented." "But is my Naikan deep enough?" The nun responds straightforwardly, "I can't get inside of you. You know best whether you have truly examined yourself." The old lady appears satisfied with the reply. Perhaps she will never realize that she and the nun spoke from different perspectives. She, of the life to come, merits and punishments in the cycle of rebirth. The nun spoke of the now.

SENKOBO—ZEN-LIKE NAIKAN

Along with Gasshoen Temple, Senkobo Temple is one of the older, established extensions of the Nara Center. Like the practitioners at Gasshoen, the Reverend Usami carries out Naikan within a religious atmosphere in a temple setting. Both temples are located in Mie Prefecture, about fifteen minutes' drive from each other. But Usami incorporates strict Zen practices within his Jodo Shinshu temple with resultant changes in Naikan style and appeal.

Zen-like practice begins even before Naikan is initiated for most of the high school disciplinary problems who are sent to Senkobo. The boys' heads are shaved and they are sent to wait outside the temple until they have demonstrated their determination to work hard at meditation. "Niwazume" in Zen practice are aspiring young monks who must wait outside the temple gates until they are permitted to enter. The niwazume at Senkobo may wait as long as ten days, without bathing, in rain or snow, before they are allowed to come into the temple during the day for Naikan. They may sleep inside at night and seek shelter under overhanging eaves to escape the elements. On the average, however, niwazume status continues for about three days at Senkobo. During that time the young men may listen to Naikan tapes and sit in private self-reflection. They also have a sheet of paper with temple rules printed on it. The rules forbid talking, walking around, writing graffiti, going outside, and loaning or borrowing money, among other restrictions. The prospective Naikansha is to learn the rules, think about them, and sign the sheet before entering.

The mensetsu at Senkobo appears to be a hybrid between the standard Naikan mensetsu and a private audience (*dokusan*) with a Zen master. Usami, sitting cross-legged with eyes nearly closed, wordlessly jangles a small bell. The first Naikansha rises from his position in line, approaches the priest, bows, and kneels on the hardwood floor. He recites his reflections. Usami listens impassively, then asks if there are questions, or he skips that query and assigns the next topic. Then, without further formality, he picks up the bell signaling that client to retreat and the next to appear.

At Senkobo the Zen influence is reflected in other practices as well. In place of the morning and evening broadcast of Naikan tapes used in Nara there is a short *kowa*, a Buddhist lecture. The themes vary but include philosophical and practical matters. For example, Zen Buddhist concepts of time, space, and history were discussed in one kowa, as were the proper ways of walking and of opening and closing doors. At another lecture Usami spoke of not "killing" (wasting) water or electricity. One must allow even an object to "use its life." At these services there are also song chants, rapid reading in unison, and repetitious recitations of the *nembutsu* (a short phrase indicating praise and dependence on Amidha Buddha).

The meals are taken in Zen temple style: served in ritual form, meatless, rapidly eaten, with bowls cleaned in prescribed manner by each participant. The business of eating takes little time but full attention. Soon the client is back to his Naikan reflection.

The *keisaku*, a flat board used in Zen training, is used to slap the backs and shoulders of clients to provide stimulation for muscles weary from sitting and to maintain alertness. A byobu screen can be opened suddenly at any time to reveal the meditating Naikansha. Without warning one must be ready at every moment to respond to a query about one's reflections. Usami cites the historic training of swordsmen to be alert at every moment for the master's sharp slap or sudden pounce. This attitude and technique contrasts with the preparatory calling of the client's name and pause before each mensetsu at Yoyogi (see below) so that the client has time to ready himself for the exchange with the therapist. The Nara Center is intermediate between the two in that the slight rustling of clothes, the soft sounds of approaching footsteps, sounds of nearby mensetsu, and the ritual bowing give the Naikansha at Nara some time to organize his thoughts and sitting posture for mensetsu. Finally, the Zen *kinhin*, a sort of continuing meditation while walking in a prescribed manner, is interspersed throughout the day to give the Naikansha relief from hours of sitting. Some form of acceptable exercise is provided in every Naikan setting.

Naikan practice at Senkobo is severe but not without warmth. If most Naikan therapists are motherlike in their gentle humility, Usami is the stern Japanese father, a model the tough young delinquents can identify with and imitate. The sternness has a loving purpose.

Usami sees four goals of Naikan practice: first is salvation; second is development and deepening of Buddhist character; third is improvement of life problems, whether psychological or social—tension, quarrels, or weak will; the fourth purpose is simply to be interesting. He sees three major results from Naikan meditation: body-mind development, self-discovery, and service to others.

Interestingly, Usami—the priest—commutes into town daily to teach junior high school. The extra income was necessary to support a building program at the temple. Usami withdrew the temple from dependence on denominational and local support and authority. It is an independent religious unit with the freedom and financial difficulties such status implies in Japan.

Usami is assisted in running the temple operation by one or two young men, his wife, and his mother-in-law. His wife is skilled in acupuncture and acupressure, sometimes treating Naikansha. She is also a dedicated Naikan practitioner. It is said that she was so deeply involved in Naikan at Yoshimoto's Nara Center that she was prevented from starving only by doctor's orders.

Usami himself will soon complete his *koan* training, thus making him fully qualified to practice both Shinshu Buddhism (for which he already had years of training and practice) and, now, Zen Buddhism.

THE MEGURO NAIKAN CENTER
WEEKEND NAIKAN

Mrs. Yoshimoto's younger sister runs a Naikan center in her home in Meguro, Tokyo. For a few years after her husband died, Mrs. Ikeda assumed the responsibility of directing his company, returning in the evenings and Sundays to do mensetsu interviews. At that time a second woman did mensetsu during the weekdays and Saturdays. Now Mrs. Ikeda devotes full time to Naikan.

Clients are relatively few. Often only one or two can be found in the newly built meditation rooms on the second floor. The modern, tatami mat rooms, one for men and one for women, are not large but are among the best furnished anywhere for Naikan. The speaker system, lighting, washroom facilities, and other details have been thoughtfully considered with Naikan in mind. Local clients may come after work on weekdays and then spend the whole day in self-reflection on weekends at the Meguro facility.

There is a quiet self-possession about Mrs. Ikeda, as if she were both wholly in this world carrying on a conversation yet simultaneously existing in some detached, distant place. Her manner seems to epitomize the effects of long hours of Naikan meditation and interviews on an introverted personality. The result is not unpleasant.

The tapes and format for mensetsu interviews in Meguro are the same as those at the Nara Center.

IBUSUKI TAKEMOTO HOSPITAL
NAIKAN FOR ALCOHOLICS

Although Takemoto Hospital is not the only Japanese facility treating alcoholics with Naikan it certainly has the longest history and most elaborate program. Dr. Takemoto has much experience working in Danshukai, Japan's Alcoholics Anonymous. In 1972 he opened his hospital with the aim of providing specialized treatment for alcoholics. In 1974 he added a new building of wards specifically for treatment of alcoholics. In the meantime Takemoto had come across a book about Naikan and had written a letter expressing his interest to Yoshimoto. A week later a large package arrived from the Nara Center with books, magazines, pamphlets, and more than fifty cassette tapes. Typical of Yoshimoto's style of giving (investing?), the unsolicited package provoked further interest and, eventually, commitment to Naikan practice at Takemoto Hospital.

The typical course of treatment for alcoholics lasts nine months (three-month and twelve-month programs have been tried; six to nine months seem optimal). The program begins with a drying-out period in an isolation cell. High on the walls of the cell, speakers broadcast tapes about alcoholism, recordings of Naikan mensetsu, and popular songs. (A behaviorist colleague of mine interspersed cartoons as reinforcers in his slide presentations of course material to medical students. Popular songs probably have the same effect here, although isolation makes almost any stimulus desirable.) This isolation period is also used as an impetus in establishing a positive relationship between therapist and future Naikansha. Periodic visits by staff members are welcome breaks in the monotony. When the therapist thinks the time is right, he gives a notebook and pen to the isolated patient. With these, the patient writes a diary of his recalled past.

The next step for the patient is a general psychiatric ward, then a locked alcoholics' ward, then an open ward for alcoholics only. By this time six months have passed. In all the alcoholics' wards speakers high on the walls play music and Naikan tapes. One hour (1:00–2:00 P.M.) is set aside each day for silent Naikan meditation. Patients from open and locked wards attend a weekly in-hospital Danshukai (AA) meeting. A typical meeting begins with an opening statement by an elected patient leader, a few minutes of silent meditation, introduction of new members, histories of their alcoholism read by several patients followed by questions from Dr. Takemoto, summaries of their week of Naikan by patients who recently completed that experience, a summary statement about the meeting, a lecture by the hospital director, and closing meditation. The Naikan summaries are the reported results of ten days of intensive Naikan. They take about two minutes each to read but are followed by severe direct questioning by Takemoto: "How much did you spend on *sake* (rice wine) during those years? Ten million yen? That's enough to buy a house. When were you separated from your children? Do you get letters from them? Are you lonely? They may be even more lonely without a father." (He turns to the assembly.) "This man could be making six million yen a year as a ball player; now even his clothes are given to him" (the hundred or so patients assembled laugh, as does the patient to whom he refers). Turning to another patient Takemoto says, "Here we have the case of a sixty-three-year-old mother taking care of her thirty-eight-year-old son. It is just the opposite of the way things should be." Another patient recounts what he lost because of alcohol as Takemoto lists the items on the blackboard: wife and child, money, family relations, work, girl friend (?!), himself. "Anything else?" "That's about all," the fellow replies sheepishly and all laugh. But the impact is serious and strong. And those who will do Naikan reflection later are learning about the proper Naikan behavior and attitude beforehand.

Before doing shuchu Naikan a patient must attend the zadankai meeting of those who have just completed their intensive Naikan. Again, information about acceptable effort is passed along and the patient may be further motivated to do deep Naikan upon hearing the experiences of his peers.

At last the patient begins the extended period of Naikan. At Takemoto Hospital it lasts for ten days (a regular course of seven-day Naikan is provided nonalcoholics from the outside community). In 1976, a new structure was built just for Naikan therapy. There, some five patients at a time do Naikan. They arise in the open ward at

5:00, work in the garden until 5:30, then sit at Naikan until 7:00 P.M., when they return to the ward to sleep. Although Takemoto has sent thirty of his fifty-five staff members to Yoshimoto's center to do Naikan, only five actually do mensetsu in Ibusuki. These staff members serve food to the Naikansha behind the byobu just as food is served at the Nara Center.

The themes of meditation are typical ones. The patient begins reflecting on his mother or mother surrogate. Later, he may move on to "lies and stealing," to calculating how much was spent on his education and food as a child, how much he spent on alcohol, and so forth. Naikan tapes are played at intervals during the day. Mensetsu behavior is standard, with admonitions to "dig deeply," "you may die any second," references to Mother's Day, etc. Both male and female staff members do mensetsu interviewing.

Patients attend biweekly meetings of Danshukai outside the hospital following Naikan. The aim is to provide a smooth transition between hospital and community life. Just before leaving the hospital a *sobetsu-kai* (farewell celebration) is held. The celebration solidifies socially the changes that have taken place in the patient. Again, the patient publicly discusses the problems that brought him to the hospital. His peers offer advice and good wishes. The doctor congratulates him and offers a final lecture. ("It may take six months to a year to change your image at home." "These will be rough times for you.") The departing patient gives a final speech. Around the table each in turn sings a song. The entire session is taped, and the patient takes with him this concrete expression of love and resolve as he leaves the hospital.

A remarkable cure rate for alcoholics of 66 percent over at least a two-year period demonstrates the effectiveness of this Naikan-centered treatment program.

MINAMI TOYOTA HOSPITAL
MORE NAIKAN FOR ADDICTION

Minami Toyota Hospital in Aichi Prefecture treats alcoholics and other addicts in a form similar to that of Kagoshima's Ibusuki Hospital. There is no separate building for Naikan at Minami Toyota; however, a couple of rooms in one ward are set aside for this treatment form. Each morning patients arise at 5:00, clean their rooms, and meditate until the first mensetsu at 9:00. During the day mensetsu responsibilities rotate among four shidosha. The format for these sessions is the same as that of Nara but they last longer—perhaps ten minutes each. Because there are rotating shidosha, each therapist enters comments on a chart in order to maintain continuity. During the last mensetsu at 5:00 P.M., meditation assignments are made to cover the period until the next mensetsu in the morning. Sundays are particularly difficult because staffing is minimal. A followup series of Saturday meetings in Alcoholics Anonymous style is the supplement to a regular course of shuchu Naikan in this setting.

Between 1976 and 1977 some fifty patients were treated with Naikan (most with tranquilizing medication, too). About 10 percent quit without completing the week. Perhaps 20 percent continued to be dry and to attend the Saturday meetings. Others lost contact with the hospital, but the staff estimated that, overall, half of those treated were helped significantly.

In its current form Naikan practice is not economically profitable at this hospital, although it is reported that the serious practice of self-reflection contributes to the positive atmosphere in the psychiatric ward. Thus Naikan seems to influence indirectly the attitudes of other patients, as well.

G.L.A. NAIKAN

Two of the newer, fast-growing facilities in Tokyo are connected with the new religion called G.L.A. (Golden Light Association) founded by the charismatic Takahashi Shinji. The recent death of the founder with subsequent dwindling of his followers from a reputed one hundred thousand to about ten thousand led some leaders to search for a firm practice to support the movement. In Naikan they found a meditative method that could be done by lay people as well as priests; in Naikan they perceived a way to regroup their resources.

The Yoyogi Naikan Center is run by the Reverend Harada, his wife, and a number of female assistants. Harada has a strong presence, commanding attention by his educated, refined manner. In addition to Naikan he uses counseling, acupuncture, and G.L.A. practices such as the laying on of hands. He reports that he is able to see psychic auras and is capable of communicating with the evil spirits that possess some neurotics.

Most of the clients at this conveniently located and well-equipped center are sent by the main temple of G.L.A., where Harada spends half of his time. Characteristic of the mensetsu interview at Yoyogi is the preparatory calling of the client's name and a greeting before the byobu screen is opened. Printed forms provide a standard format for the guide and client during mensetsu. Other forms show the fixed daily schedule and the bathing order and times. The overall impression is a facility run efficiently, presenting a polished image.

The Koganei Family Naikan Center is run by the Reverend Haba and his staff. Haba is a skilled family counselor with a warm, persuasive voice and a fine listening manner. At Koganei the treatment emphasis is on having the whole family do Naikan whenever possible. Thus, not only do the individual members change, but so does the environment in which they interact daily.

At this center it is suggested that the parents of a problem child do Naikan first. Then the young person comes for self-reflection. While the youth is doing Naikan, his parents write letters to him at least twice. These letters contain expressions of their love for him and their hopes for his future. Few Japanese youth have received such frank and direct communications on these subjects from their parents. The impact of reading the letters moves the young person into deeper Naikan.

Another feature of this setting is the scheduling of thirty-minute exercise periods each morning and afternoon. There is debate in Naikan circles about the value of such exercise—whether it contributes to concentration or distracts from it.

The day at Koganei begins at 6:00 A.M. and ends at 10:00 P.M.; thus it is shifted to a schedule one hour later than that at Nara. One may begin intensive Naikan any day of the week, continue day by day, or arrange for periods of up to a month. However, as in most settings, one week is usual. There are three interviewers at this facility, all living on the grounds or nearby and handling up to twenty-five clients. The interviews characteristically run somewhat longer than those at Nara, perhaps 20 to 30 percent longer.

Here, too, acupuncture is used as an adjunct therapy, as are other forms of Chinese medicine. Depressed and schizophrenic patients are sometimes accepted if their disturbance is adequately controlled by medication.

It is apparent that the leaders at both of these G.L.A.-related facilities have used the organizational skills and resources available to them to found stable Naikan centers which were utilized immediately by their believer clients. Thus, the usual initial difficulties of capital investment and of building up a practice have been largely eliminated in these circumstances.

The Kibo Club
Businessman's Naikan

Yanagida San is in the trading business. His is an active, demanding occupation. Yet Yanagida San is also Yanagida Sensei, the founder of a Naikan practice center in downtown Tokyo. On the seventh floor of a modern building near the Meijiza Performing Arts Center is a room thirty meters square with a modest sign marking it as the Kibo (Hope) Club.

There, two Sundays each month, a few at a time, people come to do Naikan. Some two hundred people over the first two years took advantage of these facilities. A fee that is the equivalent of about ten dollars covers the cost of guided Naikan meditation, a *sushi* lunch, a bath, training in some basic relaxation and massage techniques from yoga, and a closing discussion period that sometimes extends well into the night. The form is flexible and broadly directed at working males in their thirties and forties, who make up about three-quarters of the clientele.

Yanagida is an energetic man dedicated to promoting self-development in the business world. He puts about a tenth of his business income into the operation of the club and the publication of a Naikan magazine. This is better than drinking away the money, he says. In addition to managing the club, Yanagida lectures about Naikan to religious groups several times each month and counsels Naikansha and their families during their readjustment in the post-Naikan period. He also attends yoga meetings at the Kibo Club several times each week.

To sustain this torrid pace Yanagida has his own program of daily Naikan. For thirty minutes each day, on the commuter train, he sits with hands clasped doing Naikan. Each morning he raises his hands to the sun for fifteen minutes or so to feel its warmth, a gift offered to many but appreciated by only a few. Deep breathing, a drink of pure water, and some time spent viewing a natural phenomenon (a bird, a flower, a tree) further promote a sense of gratitude for the life he has been given. Daily yoga exercises round out his program of self-development.

Yanagida considers the three Naikan questions—What did I receive? What did I give? What trouble did I cause?—to be as applicable to the environment as to the social relationships usually considered by Naikan people. With an appreciation of the sun, water, air, plant and animal life, and one's own body, one naturally checks any impulses to pollute or damage one's world.

Like many others who carry out aftercare in some form, Yanagida is convinced that the real fruits of Naikan may take a year or more of daily attention to this lifeway in order to ripen. Periodic "booster shots" of intensive Naikan on a biweekly basis help sustain the Naikansha in his efforts to build a life of gratitude and service.

THE SAPPORO NAIKAN ZENDO
ECLECTICISM AND NAIKAN

From the southernmost tip of Kyushu, Naikan extends to the northernmost main island, Hokkaido. There in the island's largest city, Sapporo, is to be found another variety of Naikan practice.

Igarashi Sensei, like Yoshimoto Sensei and Yanagida Sensei (and like Werner Erhard of est), came out of the business world to practice therapy. As company head Igarashi had joined a counseling group in order to learn how to advise his employees. He came to see his own need for further guidance, dropped from the company, and entered the Buddhist priesthood for three years. In the meantime his wife and three sons waited patiently for the deepened and enlightened Igarashi to return.

The outcome of his training is a flexible Naikan-style fitted within a larger program of therapy which takes place in essentially three steps. The first step in Igarashi's ten-day course of treatment is a sort of nondirective counseling. The client needs to talk, to be heard, to be understood. Igarashi listens for hour after hour as the patient elects to pour out his troubles, his complaints, his past failures. The Sensei listens. And a relationship of trust develops. This period may last from one to four days but averages about two days. The counseling sessions are taped.

The second step is one of self-examination. Basically, the format is the same one-week Naikan course as that at the Nara Center (where both Igarashi and his wife have done a week of shuchu Naikan). The tapes played for the Naikansha during this period are the standard ones created by Yoshimoto, but also the tapes of the previous hours of counseling are played over and over at least four or five times so that the client can hear himself and deepen his self-examination. The mensetsu interviews run somewhat longer in this setting than in Nara.

The third step takes the client beyond self-understanding and helps him determine how to live from the newly gained perspective. To this end zazen, yoga, and light hypnotic states are employed. The client who feels guilty after Naikan, for example, is taught the Theravada Buddhist technique of looking at his guilt from a detached third-person perspective and so is enabled to separate his action-self from the feeling. The person who realizes how much others have done for him may discover through zazen that he and those others are one, that the separation between self and other is a sort of fiction. Hypnosis is used to plant suggestions of confidence, relaxation, reminders to do daily Naikan, and so forth. Yoga exercises help maintain a proper body-mind balance. (In passing, one might point out that there was a sort of yoga boom in Japan late in the 1970s, with popular magazine articles devoted to the subject and an increasing number of practitioners.)

Perhaps two-thirds of Igarashi's clients are women. The age groups in the twenties and thirties are most frequently represented. Students, office workers, and housewives—city folk—are the vast majority. At any time there are likely to be three or four clients (at the most, six) sitting each in his own room in Igarashi's home. Others come and go freely before and after the ten-day course. As Mrs. Igarashi put it,

"They are more like friends or brothers and sisters than like strangers or patients." Payment is on a voluntary basis. In the two years of practice only four or five clients have stopped treatment in mid-course and returned home. In view of the self-selection, the elaborate initial counseling period, and the flexible and warm style, this high completion rate is understandable.

Igarashi Sensei was introduced to Naikan by his friend, Usami Sensei, another Naikan therapist with training as a Zen Buddhist priest. Usami's temple practice at Senkobo was described above.

The Iwate Meetings
Group Support

In Iwate Profecture, a small group meets each month to practice Naikan in one of the members' home. Usually, there are about ten present, with two-thirds of them experienced Naikansha. The remaining guests come usually at personal invitation to learn more about Naikan. Over the two-year existence of the group, some forty to fifty people have attended at one time or another.

The meeting format has three elements. It begins with several hours of formal Naikan, the members sitting behind byobu screens or facing the wall of the house. An experienced member conducts mensetsu. Then comes an informal discussion period with, perhaps, a guest speaker. And, finally, a relaxed sharing of dinner together.

This Naikan group provides preparation, aftercare, and motivational support for daily Naikan practice. The members are clear on their main purpose—to sit in Naikan together. Among those attending, females far outnumber males, and women in their fifties form the majority (those in their forties constitute the next largest number).

At a meeting in August 1978, group members put forth several interesting comments and viewpoints. One leader noted that she is a better counselor for having done Naikan because she can better take her client's point of view. Another Naikansha pointed out that teachers with much Naikan experience need give only one answer to a student's question because they can empathize with the student's perspective and truly understand the question. Another person confessed his previous inability to meet with strangers and his new courage in that area now, thanks to Naikan. A young lady who had recently completed Naikan at Nara found her relationships somewhat disrupted and her attention too much focused on rebalancing them. Experienced Naikansha told her that this self-consciousness in the giving and receiving of favors from others is a good sign—a sign that things were not as they should have been before Naikan and that Naikan had produced a profound effect on her. Sometimes it takes up to a year to feel natural in this new Naikan life-style.

Some members said they talk less after doing Naikan; some said they talk more. An office worker found that she could speak more freely after doing Naikan; particularly her morning greeting to others at the office came naturally now. A first-time visitor tearfully spoke of her difficulty with two children who refused to go to school. Immediate support followed as a veteran member related that she had become interested in Naikan because of the same problem. She pointed out another group member who also shared difficulties with her children. Another woman confessed that, during Naikan, she discovered that *she* was her child's problem. How very Naikan-like. As Mizuno put it, "The child is the mirror of the parent."

NAIKAN IN PENAL INSTITUTIONS

Kitsuse's early reports on Naikan (1965, 1968) emphasized the ties between self-reflection and prisoner reform. At the time of Kitsuse's writing Yoshimoto had received the greatest acceptance for his method within the criminal rehabilitation system. Naikan's beginnings in Japan's penal system can be traced to Yoshimoto's lecture at Nara Prison in March 1954.

Kitsuse was impressed that Naikan assumed even criminals to be fundamentally moral, social beings. A true sociopath, outside the moral system, would be unwilling and unable to do genuine Naikan. To the sociopath, the self-attribution of having done wrong to others would be so many words, nothing more. Kitsuse points out that Naikan assumes the criminal has done wrong and has been isolated and confined because he has failed to meet his moral obligations toward other members of society. Acknowledging his misdeeds, acknowledging and appreciating the legitimacy of others' claims on him and service to him, repenting, and resolving to serve others is the recognized path of rehabilitation.

In the prison that Kitsuse observed there was a thirty-minute briefing of Naikan candidates. The briefing included a description of the Naikan method and some warning about the usual initial difficulties in concentrating and remembering. Some authority-figure such as the warden would praise those who volunteered and encourage them to persist. Naikan was often conducted in the cells, with the meditator facing a blank wall. Guards with personal Naikan experience conducted the periodic mensetsu. At the end of the six to ten days of Naikan a badge was awarded and the prisoners were admonished not to soil the reputation of Naikan and their sensei guide.

Typical reflections of attitude changes during Naikan in a prison setting are these paraphrased questionnaire responses of Hiroshima delinquents (Miki 1972a). *Before Naikan*: I wasn't bad, society was; I

51

wasn't bad, my parents were; my family is uninteresting; I have no feeling of apology to my family; I'm angry at my keepers; raising children is the mother's responsibility; it's all right if I live or die; forget about it, I tell myself, and don't mention my past misdeeds to any one. *During Naikan*: I've come to dislike myself; I feel small; ashamed, guilty toward my parents; I caused trouble for my parents, especially Mother; I realize my own badness; I'm surprised at how much bad I've done; I'm upset at my terrible deeds; I hope to change myself by Naikan, become more human; I feel deep gratitude; no one held back from me, *I* was bad; I'm grateful that a person like me was allowed to live; I'll straighten up day by day.

During the heyday of Naikan in prisons a number of studies were conducted on recidivism rates. As shown in table 5 Naikan was consistently associated with significantly lowered rates of return to prison following release.

The problem in interpreting these data, of course, lies in the self-selection of prison candidates for Naikan. Self-reflection was conducted on a voluntary basis. Perhaps many of those who were good reform risks anyway were among the ones who asked for Naikan.

Naikan has had its ups and downs during its twenty-five years in Japan's penal institutions. In 1959 some 14 prisons and 6 reform schools had Naikan programs (Takeda 1978). In June 1962, 29 of 60 prisons and 10 of 61 juvenile reform schools used Naikan, but in March 1971 only 5 prisons, 2 reform schools, and 1 detention/evaluation facility used Naikan (Takeda 1971). In 1973 Naikan, on the rise again, was practiced in 7 prisons and 10 juvenile rehabilitation facilities. Narita (1978) reported 15 of 21 juvenile detention facilities using Naikan in 1978. Takeda (1978) predicts increasing use of this method throughout Japan's penal system in the 1980s.

What factors have contributed to this roller-coaster effect on Naikan's popularity in these institutions? Much of the initial success can be attributed to Yoshimoto's charisma and persistence. Newspaper articles, radio broadcasts, and public lectures stirred interest in Naikan as a reform method that changed the criminal's heart. Dedicated prison guards and higher officials tried Naikan themselves and observed its effects on inmates. The Naikan movement in prison settings spread in concentric circles from the Nara area.

But as time passed criticisms began to appear. These criticisms were of three sorts: ideological, political, and practical. Ideologically, the religious trappings of Naikan clashed with the penal system's aim of scientific reform of prisoners. Issues were raised related to infiltration of a government institution by Jodo Shinshu Buddhism. Yoshimoto began to appear in newspaper photos less frequently wearing the black robes of a priest and more often in a business suit. But the public image of Naikan was already established and was hard to reframe within more secular contours.

Politics, too, entered the picture, causing Naikan's decline in popularity in the late 1960s and early 1970s. Naikan was conducted, for the most part, by low-status personnel—guards. Aside from permitting the practice, high-level prison officials usually had nothing else to do with Naikan. Their distance from and lack of knowledge about Naikan practice made them vulnerable to criticisms leveled by jealous power groups within the prison system. Those who practiced Naikan had no organization or power to maintain their position, only a loose network of informal ties through Yoshimoto.

Specific practical criticisms included the difficulties of pulling guards away from other duties to do Naikan interviews, the evasion of prison work for one week by those prisoners who chose to do Naikan, the problems of time, money, and curriculum for training guards to become Naikan guides, and the absence of strong evidence for the long-term effectiveness of the method on prison populations.

The recent resurgence of Naikan in some prisons and especially in juvenile rehabilitation facilities can be attributed, in all likelihood, to changes both in Japan's penal system and in Naikan itself. The justice system in Japan, like that of the United States, has moved toward shorter prison sentences. This means that rehabilitation, if it is to occur at all, must be compacted into intensive, short-term periods. Naikan has just such a capacity. And Naikan itself has been evolving in ways that make it more acceptable to prison officials today than in the past.

To be sure, Naikan retains its strong religious flavor in temples at Gasshoen and Senkobo and has adapted even a new religious aura at G.L.A. facilities in Tokyo. However, in a sense, Yoshimoto's form of self-reflection has outgrown its priestly robes. No longer is it "merely" a path to salvation, it has become a "therapy" with implications for its status, its acceptability in secular circles, and its applicability to a wider range of troubles. As a treatment for alcoholism, neurosis, and psychosomatic disorders Naikan has achieved a new sort of respectability. *Naikan and Mental Health, Naikan Therapy, An Introduction to Naikan Therapy* are recent book titles (in Japanese) giving evidence of the new status. Physicians are increasingly interested in an indigenous treatment form for the notoriously hard to treat alcoholics. Researchers such as the renowned Professor Ikemi Yujiro of Kyushu University have come out in support of Naikan.

All this recognition contributes to Naikan's public image in the secular world and makes it more acceptable to prison officials. Now that the atmosphere has changed, there are a few ranking supporters of Naikan in the penal system who can press more effectively for pilot efforts in settings where Naikan has not yet begun.

Another factor that may be contributing to Naikan's recent success in juvenile facilities is the exploratory, experimental orientation of some guard-practitioners. The normal continuous week of Naikan is disrupted in these institutions by changes of shift, night cell-lockup, weekends off, vacations, and other staff duties. Such features have spurred innovation. For example, various periods of meditation have been tried, including shorter daily self-reflection periods of up to twenty days. Other innovations include the use of written diaries or logs, unique question-and-answer formats for mensetsu, written questionnaires for inmates, and checkoff sheets of progress filled out by staff and returned as feedback to inmates. The effectiveness of these tactics has yet to be assessed; at present, however, they made Naikan possible in situations that might otherwise preclude the practice in its original form.

Narita (1978) conducted a survey of the practice and problems of Naikan in Japan's penal system. Tokyo's Tama Juvenile Facility conducts Naikan from 7:00 A.M. to 9:00 P.M. using two therapists. There is difficulty providing Naikan supervision on weekends and holidays. At the Nara Juvenile Facility Naikan is normally conducted three times for each inmate, at arrival, midpoint, and departure. Each Naikan sequence runs four days, from 9:00 A.M. to 4:30 P.M. each day, with a diary assignment in the evenings. During the first period the topical focus is reflection on the family and the motivations for becoming delinquent. The second period, during mid-sentence, covers current relationships with others at the Nara facility. And the final period, before release, emphasizes preparation for life on the outside. At the Kono Women's Facility Naikan is conducted for only three days, from 9:00 A.M. to 12:30 P.M. There, twice a year, a meeting is held for inmates to present publicly accounts of their experiences with the method.

From Narita's own experience with Naikan at Hokkaido Juvenile Facility, he writes that no rehabilitation program, however diverse and well run, can be effective if the inmates are not motivated to participate and learn from the program. Whatever else it does, Naikan seems to be effective in creating the proper motivation for effective use of the rest of his program. At the Hokkaido facility all the inmates do daily Naikan from 6:30 to 7:00 A.M. sitting on their bunks facing the wall. They write about their reflections in a journal and are questioned daily on the contents of these journals.

Even with the increasingly favorable attitude toward this sort of rehabilitation, however, criticisms are not absent. Takeda (1978) reported questionnaire results in which 47 prison official respondents expressed doubts about the training of therapist-guards (94.5 percent), doubts about the range of types of persons who respond to the method

(42.6 percent), doubts about the long-term effectiveness of Naikan (23.4 percent), and worries about the likelihood that Naikan would produce an unhealthy self-punitiveness in the inmates (29.8 percent).

Oita Juvenile Facility
Naikan for Delinquents

The inmates of the Oita facility in Miyazaki Prefecture range from about fourteen to twenty years of age. As a result of the trend in Japan to minimize incarceration, the number of inmates has dropped from over four hundred several years ago to less than sixty in 1978. Similarly the length of stay has decreased. In this abbreviated sentence Naikan can be seen to take an increasingly important role in rehabilitation, achieving relatively powerful results in a brief period.

At Oita every inmate completes three periods of Naikan: one week shortly after admission, another in the middle of his stay, and a final week before discharge. In addition some 3 to 5 percent request additional weeks of Naikan and about 20 percent are assigned additional "special" Naikan as a result of misbehavior.

Naikan is carried out in an isolation cell about eight feet by twelve feet. In the cell is a toilet, washbasin, bedding, a small table, cushions, and a food slot. There are six such cells at Oita. Mr. Hirose is the guard with major responsibility for mensetsu of the Nakansha in these cells. He has created his own introductory tape aimed at delinquents. In addition, he uses some thirty tapes selected from the Nara collection. They are played in a prescribed order to avoid repetition because the various Naikansha begin their weeks of meditation at staggered times.

The first few days Hirose spends much mensetsu time listening to the youth, establishing a relationship, encouraging motivation. Thereafter, every two hours during his shift he conducts mensetsu for three or four minutes with each Naikansha (they are called *seito*, "students," at this facility). On Hirose's days off another guard does mensetsu or the seito write their reflections on notepaper. A daily chart is kept and points are assigned for each day's Naikan depth; lower scores may prolong the period of self-reflection. At the end of the week a mimeographed form is provided the seito for summarizing his Naikan experience. On it are such questions as: How did you think about life before doing Naikan? What were your faults? What was the best thing you did for your family in the past? What is the worst thing, the one you reflected on most? What would be the best attitude toward life from now on? What was the most upsetting thing about doing Naikan? Will you practice Naikan from now on? Did you want to cry while doing Naikan? Did you cry? What made you cry?

At Oita's juvenile detention facility Naikan is part of a larger program of rehabilitation with a regular progression toward release. Individualized written goals, counseling, and psychodrama are also part of the program. Hirose is impressed with the results, estimating that nearly 100 percent of the seito improved or greatly improved, with no significant dropout rate (2 out of 240 dropped out in 1977); this estimate is based on his experience over a five-year period in treating more than a thousand lower-class young men. Followup, however, is not possible because after the seito is released he ordinarily has no further contact with the facility.

Hirose is typical of the dedicated mensetsu guides within the Japanese penal system who work with minimal support from top-level administrators. The hope of such interviewers is that Naikan will be established on a solid scientific (rather than religious) basis and that it will be recognized as the useful rehabilitation adjunct it appears to be.

Further Variants

Naikan has been used in conjunction with other therapies, notably counseling, hypnosis, autogenic training, and various religious practices with therapeutic aspects such as zazen, chanting, and repetition of the nembutsu. Discussion of counseling and religious practices appears above in sections on specific settings where such practices occur. In this section I shall consider the combined use of Naikan, hypnosis, and autogenic training in clinical settings not covered elsewhere, as well as some specialized variations of Naikan. The aim is to round out our view of the breadth of Naikan practice.

Ishida (1969, 1972) was the first therapist to use Naikan systematically with hypnosis and autogenic training. Although he treated some patients only with hypnosis or autogenic training (a sort of self-hypnosis and structured relaxation program developed in Germany), he found it useful to use both along with Naikan for most effective results. Beginning with autogenic training, he aimed at giving the patient a sense of autonomy, of control over his functions of breathing, pulse, and relaxation. This step also prepared the patient for easier induction of hypnosis, the second step. Hypnosis was used to examine the depth of the client's psychological disturbance through regression and catharsis. Ishida's interpretations addressed to the patient were broadly psychoanalytic in nature, covering dreams, blocking, and the like. Posthypnotic suggestions were made to relieve distracting symptoms and to prepare the client for Naikan. Ishida (1969) reported an effectiveness of over 90 percent for this method, a report based on his clinical judgment. Psychosomatic problems and anxiety neuroses seemed most amenable to this treatment form though a variety of neurotics were treated.

More recently, Kishioka (1978) uses hypnosis in what he calls "trance Naikan." He meets with the patient one hour a week, induces hypnotic trance, and regresses the patient to do Naikan reflection on earlier periods of his life. For some patients the regression seems to break through the defenses against remembering past misdeeds. Kishioka may send patients for longer periods of intensive Naikan to other centers. Hypnosis can be used to increase the motivation for doing Naikan, to reduce intrusive stray thoughts, to aid the patient in adapting to the restrictive Naikan milieu, and to reduce ego defensiveness.

Kishioka, like Ishida, uses hypnosis and Naikan within a broader treatment framework. In this case, the treatment involves counseling, repetition of phrases such as "Everything is all right as it is," physical exercises, breath training, and teaching an overall philosophy built on the premise that "I *am* my neighbor."

At Okayama University Naikan becomes one part of a daily activity program for some psychiatric inpatients. On discharge the self-reflection is carried out at home for two hours both in the morning and in the afternoon, with daily visits to the hospital to report on the meditation's progress. The treatment gradually tapers off to a single daily Naikan-focused conversation between the patient and his mother. This feature, involving progressive steps in an overall program which includes Naikan, is similar to that found in the alcohol treatment programs and criminal rehabilitation programs described above.

Specific sorts of patient problems have provoked development of special Naikan programs to meet these needs. Mensetsu sequences have been designed particularly for alcoholics, persons with marital problems, daughters-in-law, and failures in love. An example of such a schedule for brokenhearted young ladies is found in Yoshimoto (1972). After the initial sequence of reflection on family members, with a repetition of the mother theme, comes, in order, reflection on schoolteachers, the amount of money the parents have spent on raising the person in question, the father (for a second time), the use of parents' money and objects without permission, stealing from others, same-sex friends, opposite-sex friends, rivals, did she act properly (toward her schoolmates, mother, lover), the value of life, did she steal from others (for a second time), the boss at her part-time work, her fellow workers, her customers, teachers, grandmother, neighbors, uncle and aunt, cousin, mother, did she steal from others including her parents (for a third time), did she do other bad things, and (again) her rivals in the past. This program lasts seven days. Of course, when reflecting on the rival theme the Naikansha is instructed to view herself as the rival saw her; always the emphasis is on what she herself contributed to hurt the rival and what the other person did to help and support her despite her negative efforts. Note that the lost lover theme covers only a very small period of reflection. Three periods of reflection on stealing change her view of herself from victim (her man was stolen) to thief. Furthermore, the experience of heartbreak is placed in the larger perspective of surrounding, giving others.

As practiced in Nara and Meguro, for example, Naikan is a time-consuming, economically difficult enterprise. Mrs. Ikeda must rush to do shopping and cooking between mensetsu interviews which continue throughout the day. Yoshimoto Sensei must have full time assistance as well as part-time help from among the Naikansha themselves to complete mensetsu in a reasonable span to time. Efforts have been made to streamline the mensetsu exchange in order to make the therapist's time-involvement minimal and efficient. To be sure, something is lost in the following shortcuts. How much is lost and whether the loss is worth the increased number of clients who can be treated remains to be seen.

Some facilities cut face-to-face interviews to a minimum by using written communications. Journals or even mimeographed forms with open-ended questions are used to supplement or to replace face-to-face contact. Bedridden patients can do Naikan through correspondence, sending an account of their reflections by mail for the therapist's comments and guidance.

Murase, in treating a Western client, had the man meditate at home. When Murase was unable to be there in person for the mensetsu, he telephoned. Extensive use of the telephone and audio tapes sent by mail or dropped off at the therapist's office by a relative or friend have yet to be developed fully by therapists, yet they seem to be options with potential. The use of audio tape seems particularly promising; for some Naikansha at Nara who are having their mensetsu recorded it is as if they were attending at least as much to the microphone and machine as to the presence of a human listener.

In this chapter I have chosen not to write about Naikan in companies and schools. In those settings Naikan has become little practiced in recent years. It will probably continue to decline there because of the potential dangers of exploitation of employees and students and the general current disaffection in Japan with spiritual training in such contexts.

PERMISSIBLE HETEROGENEITY

It is important to consider which aspects of a therapy permit more flexibility and which permit less. Such consideration allows us to determine the therapy forms that are seen to be effective and essential from the perspective of the therapists. Examination of the kinds and degrees of flexibility permitted also dispels the doubts of some Westerners about the severity of the method. Much more leeway is permitted in practice than appears in the brief descriptions of Naikan that have appeared in English.

Unlike the postures for zazen and seiza, the sitting posture of Naikan meditation is freely selected by the Naikansha. The Nara facility ostensibly prohibits only lying down (for fear of dozing), and some other Naikan settings are even less strict. People with leg cramps or other physical disabilities may be encouraged to lie down in special rooms provided for such a posture. And, in fact, every Naikan facility has Naikansha meditating while standing, sitting, and lying down. The settings vary in the type and number of pillows provided for the Naikansha's comfort. At Nara, for example, each client has at least one flat square pillow and one round tufted one (of the sort used in some Zen temples).

Meals vary in number and content and style of service. Each day in a dining hall Gasshoen serves two meatless meals featuring unpolished rice. Takemoto Hospital serves three meals per day with meals eaten behind the byobu screen (as is the practice at the Nara Center). These choices are determined neither by the number of meditators nor the space available, although the dining-hall form is clearly more efficient (in terms of staff effort) once the number of Naikansha exceeds two or three.

The client is free to leave his place of meditation as often as he wishes to wash face and hands, brush teeth, go to the toilet, do hand laundry, and so forth. The general principle seems to be that as long as the Naikansha does not unduly disturb others and does give the slightest indication that he is making some effort to do Naikan his behavior will be tolerated (far beyond the point at which many American therapeutic staff members would begin to complain loudly).

There is variety in terms of the length of the total period of intensive self-reflection, the length of the mensetsu interviews and the intervals between them, and whether or not the client is required to or permitted to write about his reflection.

Most facilities have a group meeting after the week, some do not. Some use Naikan audio tapes; others do not. In some facilities smoking is permitted (cigarettes may even be sold); in other settings it is forbidden. Additional areas of flexibility may be found in the descriptions provided above of specific Naikan facilities.

The less flexible rules are simply stated and often are written in this form:

1. Do not leave the facility.
2. Do not emerge from behind the byobu except for going to toilet, bath, or bed.

3. Do not talk with other Naikansha.
4. Do not read, watch television, or listen to the radio.
5. Do not contact the outside world by phone or letter.

There are additional rules, less formally stated, but operating nevertheless. Appear to be making an effort to do Naikan; sleep, eat, and bathe at assigned times; do not spend a lot of time rummaging through luggage; do not doze off during the day; do not deviate excessively from the format of mensetsu; do not allow emotional involvement (e.g., tears) or noninvolvement (e.g., boredom) to interfere with Naikan reflection. In sum, rules are aimed at reducing the impact of all stimuli except those directly related to the Naikan reflection process.

Rule-breaking often implies some associated punishment. Punishment can be defined in many ways. Often it is a response by authority figures to misbehavior of a social inferior. Usually the response has some painful or restricting element. Interestingly, once in a while one comes across responses that appear to be punishing yet are explicitly defined as something else. At Takemoto Hospital rule-breaking may result in the patient's being put back in isolation (no smoking is permitted there) for one week. The purpose is said to be "self-reflection," not punishment. Similarly, a patient may be sent back from the open ward to the locked ward until he develops better "self-control." That response, also, is defined by staff as character education rather than punishment. At Oita Juvenile Facility "special" Naikan may be the consequence of misbehavior. Then, in a small isolation cell, the patient is assigned topics of self-examination for a week. Again, my direct questioning of prison guards produced explicit denial that staff or inmates consider "special" Naikan to be a form of punishment.

Such selective definitions of what appear to be classic rule-breaking punishment circumstances are not so unusual in Japan. In the past the painful practice of moxibustion or burning of moxa powder on an acupuncture site was forced on misbehaving Japanese children in order to help them develop a better character. Again, punishment was not considered by many parents to be the motive, although some children considered it such.

3 _____ Questionnaire Research

Two questionnaires were constructed during the months preceding my 1978 field trip to Japan. In Japan the translation and refining of the items progressed. Final wording and a few additional questions were suggested by Yoshimoto Sensei. The questionnaires, in English translation, are reproduced in Appendixes B and C.

The questionnaires were printed in Nara and mailed from the Naikan Training Center in Koriyama. They contained a note from Mr. Yoshimoto requesting cooperation and stating a deadline for returns some three months later. The returns, too, were to be funneled through the Nara Naikan Training Center. Every major setting in which intensive (shuchu) Naikan was practiced received the question-naire packet.

The packet itself contained copies of both questionnaires—one for therapists and one for Naikansha. All therapists and all Naikansha were asked to provide the requested information for a specified three-month period. Responses from Naikansha and from therapists were received from seven settings: Nara, Senkobo, Meguro, Gasshoen, Yoyogi, Ibusuki and Minami Toyota. In addition, responses by thera-pists alone came from an Iwate Prefecture group leader and from the therapist-guard at Oita Reform School. These replies represent all of the oldest established Naikan centers and a good cross-sectional repre-sentation of the newer extensions of Naikan (see Chapter 2).

CLIENT QUESTIONNAIRE

In general, two sorts of information were sought by means of the questionnaires for Naikansha. The first sort of descriptive analysis involved comparisons among Naikansha in the different settings. In what ways are the clients who come for treatment to Nara like those who come to Gasshoen or Ibusuki, for example, and in what ways are they different? The second sort involved pooling the data from all settings in order to examine general relationships between, say, the depth of Naikan and the age of the client or between family structure and ability to accept a Naikan perspective about the world.

Descriptive Tabulations

Data are presented in tables 6 through 13. Numbers of cases vary from table to table due to missing data. The eighteen cases from Minami Toyota Hospital are not included in the analysis because they were not collected during the comparable three-month time period. In all tables the overall differences among settings are significant beyond the .001 level using chi square analysis. That is, the chi square value for each table as a whole is beyond the .001 level.

From table 6 it is clear that the Naikan settings have clientele in a variety of age-group patterns. Nearly half of Senkobo's clients were under twenty, and nearly 40 percent of Gasshoen's Naikansha were at least sixty years old. Over half of the patients at Ibusuki Hospital were in their forties. Nara showed a clientele fairly well balanced across age groups.

Focus on particular age groups allows some specialization in method. Gasshoen has a building set aside for elderly Naikansha with physical disabilities, for example, and Senkobo can require Zen-like austerities from the young males who seek treatment there.

From a look at the numbers of elder and younger brothers and sisters in each setting it would appear that the clients at Nara, Senkobo, and Meguro tended to come from smaller families. But since these sibling variables are all highly correlated with age (r beyond .3) they probably only represent the differences among the age groups in these settings. That is, younger Japanese tend to report having fewer siblings.

The Naikansha at Nara and Senkobo are about 2:1 male to female (table 7). Ibusuki has an even higher proportion of males, about 4:1. Yet the proportions are reversed at the remaining facilities with ratios of about 2:1 female to male. In the case of Meguro and Gasshoen, the shidosha who conduct mensetsu are all female and in Yoyogi they are female with only one exception. It would appear that the Naikan settings with more balanced sex ratios among therapists attract smaller proportions of female clients than those with exclusively (or nearly exclusively) female therapists.

Occupationally (table 8), Senkobo had the largest percentage of students (51 percent), Gasshoen the largest percentage of farmers (26 percent), Yoyogi the largest percentage of office workers (27 percent) and others (30 percent), and Ibusuki the largest percentage of unemployed. During this period Nara treated the only professional therapists (7) and nearly all of the hospital employees (23 of 24). From the variety of occupational categories, age- and sex-groups represented, it is apparent that Naikan has a fairly broad appeal within the Japanese population.

In terms of religion (table 9), Gasshoen Temple had the largest Jodo Shinshu clientele (83 percent) and treated almost no one who was not a Buddhist by self-definition. Senkobo Temple also treated few clients who were not Buddhist. In contrast, half of the clients at Meguro and nearly one-third at Ibusuki claimed no religion at all.

The urban-rural dimension is only a very rough estimate in this study (table 10). All centers treated more clients from large cities than from all other residential areas combined. However, in Yoyogi practically all clients (93 percent) were from the highly urbanized Tokyo area and, in contrast, little more than half the clients of Gasshoen (55 percent) and Ibusuki (57 percent) came from roughly comparable urban areas. The remaining settings were intermediate between these extremes.

Naikansha are likely to have some knowledge about this method before beginning treatment. Of all those queried less than 35 percent began Naikan without previously knowing anyone else who had tried it. About 18 percent knew one other person, and over half knew two or more Naikansha. Nearly 60 percent had read a book about Naikan; fewer had read magazines or heard audio tapes on the subject.

The type of referral pattern varied in characteristic ways from setting to setting (table 11). Nara, Meguro, and Ibusuki attracted about one-third of their clientele through referrals from professional therapists. Yoyogi and Gasshoen Temple relied most heavily on religious professionals to tell potential clients about Naikan. Thirty-six percent of Senkobo's young men learned about Naikan from their teachers. And 44 percent of the alcoholics at Ibusuki Hospital learned about Naikan from their friends, probably fellow patients. Yet despite the generally predictable sources of these first contacts with information about Naikan, no single source brought even half the clients to any Naikan facility. Every Naikan setting has some diversity in terms of its informational and referral resources.

Fewer than 10 percent of the clients sampled responded that there was some category of persons whom they would not want to know about their Naikan experience. This percentage includes six persons who wished to keep their Naikan secret from two categories of acquaintances. Neighbors, workmates, friends, and fellow students were the most frequently selected groups to which revelation would be undesirable. Families were very rarely selected. Thus, the stigma surrounding care for mental illness seems not to operate strongly here. Naikan's public image is more one of self-discovery and personal growth either within or outside a religious context.

Another series of questions was aimed at finding out who actually knew that the Naikansha had come for treatment and who did not know. Only 3.1 percent of the total sample responded that their families did not know, 15.7 percent reported that their friends did not know, 8.3 percent reported that fellow workers did not know, and 6.1 percent reported that their teachers did not know. So, in fact, a few more people *were not* informed about the treatment beyond those the clients felt *ought not* to be informed. Still, the percentages remain small. Many Naikansha wrote spontaneously that they wished their Naikan stay to be widely transmitted to anyone with an interest in the matter. They were proud of their achievement, perhaps, and wished to support the Naikan movement in any way possible.

What sorts of motivations provoked these people to seek Naikan? And what results did they expect? As table 12 indicates, clients in certain settings tended to have characteristic complaints. Of course, Ibusuki specializes in treatment of alcoholics, many of whom saw their problem not strictly as alcoholism but as a broader need for self-development. Yoyogi's Naikansha were primarily members of the G.L.A. religious sect. They came, in general, for self-discovery and deepening of their religious understanding. School problems characterized the motivation of most Senkobo clients. Family problems (particularly between mother-in-law and daughter-in-law), seeking of religious inspiration, and (compared with other settings) the desire to cure physical ailments characterized Gasshoen believers. Compared with other settings, Meguro and Nara had proportionately more clients who defined their problems in mental health terms, although in neither of these treatment facilities were such clients in the majority.

The results expected also varied by setting (see table 13). Compared with clients from other Naikan centers, those at Gasshoen showed high religious expectations, those at Yoyogi and Gasshoen defined some of their expectations concerning religious results in other-oriented terms (e.g., to be able to take another's point of view, to serve others, to cause them less trouble, to improve relations at home or work), those at Ibusuki expected cure of their alcoholism, and the youth at Senkobo appropriately saw themselves as students coming to learn how to do Naikan. In every setting the majority of responses to the question of expected results fell into the category called here "self-oriented." It included self-growth (over 20 percent of responses from Nara, Senkobo, and Ibusuki), deepening of one's gratitude or sense of being loved (over 20 percent of responses from Nara and Senkobo), self-discovery (over 20 percent of responses from all settings except Senkobo), as well as creating a change of attitude, developing confidence, becoming happy, and planning for the future.

Correlational Analysis

All appropriate items on the question-naires from all settings were paired for analysis by correlation. Of the 171 Spearman correlations 53 were significant beyond the .001 level. Of course, the strength of the relationships are of most interest. Of the 15 pairs with relatively strong correlations (r greater than .3) most findings were trivial (e.g., the appearance of a strong relationship between the ages of the client's father and mother, r = .95). However, certain relationships concerning the client's degree of involvement in Naikan appeared in this phase of the data analysis.

The greater the number of other persons the client knew who had done Naikan, the longer he/she had known about the therapy (r = .31) and the more books he/she had read on the subject (r = .31). Similarly, the longer the person had known about Naikan, the more books (r = .32) he/she were likely to have read. And those who read more books were also likely to have read more magazines (r = .35). Other correlations in the .2 to .3 range add to the picture of older people knowing more Naikansha, reading more about Naikan (but listening less to Naikan tapes), choosing particular settings, and scoring on various measures as doing deeper (i.e., better) Naikan.

In general, then, there is a pattern of relative immersion in Naikan by some clients. Such a constellation seems little influenced by the sex of the client or by his or her family makeup (i.e., the number of elder or younger brothers and sisters).

REGRESSION

As discussed in Chapter 1, at the Naikan center in Nara, Mr. Yoshimoto in consultation with other therapists assigns a Naikan "depth" score for each client based on a subjective evaluation of the client's overall conduct at the center and his responses during mensetsu interviews. The question arises, is there some objective criteria that will predict the client's ability to do Naikan as scored by Mr. Yoshimoto?

A regression analysis appeared to be called for in order to determine what other questionnaire items might be contributing to the variance of the depth score. With this goal in mind, a regression analysis was run on the responses to sixteen items by 155 clients from the Nara setting. Only Nara data were used because that was the only setting with depth scores. Only 155 cases had no missing data on any item in the analysis. In other words, any case which had missing data (such as a lack of response or an uncodable response) for *any* of the sixteen items was eliminated from the regression analysis. The included questionnaire items were Naikan depth (the dependent variable), an objective measure of Naikan-like responses (a total score for ten questions from Miki [1978], related to the client's perception of himself and the world—see Appendix B), the age and sex of the client, the number of elder and younger brothers and sisters, the ages of the father and mother, the level of urbanization of the client's place of residence, the number of months the client had known about Naikan, the number of persons he/she knew who had done Naikan, and the number of books read on the subject.

The results were most interesting. The variable from this set of items contributing most strongly to the variance of the depth score was the number of months the client had known about Naikan (B = .764). Thus, it appears that greater familiarity with the Naikan world view contributes to Naikan depth. Those who had known about Naikan for the longest period of time were likely to have returned for their second or third week of Naikan when they filled out the questionnaire.

The second strongest variable contributing to Naikan depth was the age of the mother (B = .469). This unexpected finding fits well within Naikan theory. The longer one's mother has been alive to care for the client the deeper should be the Naikansha's recognition of her efforts in his/her behalf. Naikan meditation on the mother is the core of this meditation form, beginning the week and occupying most of the client's time during the week. Note that the client's own age (B = − .327) and the father's age (B = − .115) were weaker contributors to the variance and were even negative in direction. Clearly, there was something unique about the relationship between the mother's age and Naikan depth for this sample.

One would wish to see these results replicated in other samples with other variable lists before placing much confidence in them. However, this analysis is an initial step in attempting to determine what factors contribute to Naikan depth scores.

Incidentally, Miki's objective measure of Naikan depth proved to be a poor predictor of Yoshimoto's depth scoring either in the regression or in the correlations, either as a combined score or broken down into self-view and world-view components. A second regression, using the Miki score as the dependent variable, showed it closely related to being a female (B = 3.40) and having an elder female sibling (B = 1.50).

Thus the two measures seem to be tapping different aspects of Naikan depth, if it is to Naikan depth at all that they are related.

Factor Analysis

Factor analysis of 148 cases from Nara with no missing data on any of twenty-three selected items was carried out. A varimax rotated factor-matrix for the questionnaire items produced little that was unexpected. The first factor showed heavy loadings on items dealing with self-image. Those who saw themselves in a positive or negative light tended to do so consistently. The Naikansha who viewed himself as warm and kind also tended to see himself as mature, honest, responsible, and forgiving. Similarly, the second factor showed consistency in social world view. The respondent who considered people to be self-seeking also considered them to be uncaring, disliking to help others, cold, and selfish.

The third factor showed very strong loadings on age of father and mother and presence of elder siblings. Less strong loadings showed for seeing the world as a caring place and doing deep Naikan. Thus, the more care-givers and the longer they live to offer that care, the more potential there appears to be for Naikan depth and world view.

The fourth factor loaded on familiarity with Naikan and Naikan depth. The principle items in this factor were the number of others known who had done Naikan, the number of Naikan books read, and Naikan depth as estimated by Yoshimoto.

THERAPIST QUESTIONNAIRE

To complement the perspective of Naikansha on the therapy, it is useful to tap the perspectives of the therapists on Naikan and on their clients. The results displayed in table 14 are based on the responses of the most experienced therapist in each setting, although each of the settings except Meguro returned questionnaires from more than one therapist (no data are available from Yoyogi). Below we shall examine all therapist responses to several other questions.

It is clear that, except for the Nara Center, Japan's Naikan facilities are relatively recently founded. Nearly all Naikan therapists had been practicing only four years or less at the time of this questionnaire and about half of them only a year or two. It is likely that in 1977 more Naikansha were treated at the Nara Center than all other Naikan facilities combined, including Japan's penal system settings.

Comparing the age and sex groupings of clients for longer periods, as estimated by the therapists, with the groupings obtained from the Naikansha respondents whose replies to the questionnaire were collected during the months of July through September 1978, (tables 6 and 7), we find few discrepancies in the Nara, Senkobo, and Ibusuki data. The estimates from these therapists were based on actual counts from existing records. The Meguro Naikansha sample of thirteen was too small to show a consistent pattern in age and sex. The Minami Toyota data (N = 18 cases) from a wider time period arrived too late to be included in the data analysis of Naikansha questionnaires and so cannot be compared. The Gasshoen data show the most interesting differences between the therapists' perspectives on who they had treated over a four-year period and the actual sample that answered the Naikansha questionnaire at Gasshoen during the summer months of 1978. The estimates and respondents breakdowns by sex are almost identical. Essentially, the discrepancy is that the sampled group of Naikansha who responded to the summer questionnaire are heavily skewed toward older age groups. The two Gasshoen therapists' estimates showed a much more symmetrical distribution, with highest frequencies of treated clients in the 30-39 and 40-49 age groups. The differences are hard to explain. During my visits to Gasshoen in summer and fall, 1978, the predominance of elderly clientele was much in evidence. Perhaps their numbers are underestimated by the therapists, who relied on memory rather than a record count for their estimates in this case.

The various Naikan facilities do show a range of social classes among the clientele treated. The subjective estimate of 20 percent upper-class clients at Gasshoen may be somewhat high. Naikansha are most likely to come from middle and lower classes in all settings. Occupations of Naikansha show a range paralleling that of the questionnaire sample. Settings have characteristic occupational backgrounds among their clientele. For example, Gasshoen has relatively greater percentages of housewives and farmers, Senkobo has relatively more students, the two alcoholism treatment facilities have large numbers of unemployed or marginally employed clients, while Nara and Meguro show a wider spectrum and balance of occupational groups.

The period of Naikan varies from one hour to one month in actuality among these settings. However, about a week of meditation is typical in all of them. Before the week is completed the percentage of clients who stop Naikan varies from virtually zero to an estimated 20 percent, although scrutiny of the records at Nara would place the figure closer to 30 percent. This variation reflects the type of clients who come or are sent to each setting, the degree of formal and informal coercion and environmental control exerted by the therapist, and the flexibility and styles of Naikan permitted in each facility.

Some facilities pull their clientele primarily from the local area (Minami Toyota, Ibusuki, Meguro, and, to a lesser degree, Gasshoen). The Nara Center is the oldest and best-known Naikan facility, drawing its Naikansha from throughout the country with referrals from a variety of sources. Gasshoen depends mostly upon family referrals and contacts in the Buddhist community. Senkobo has numerous school referrals. Various paths lead the alcoholic to the hospitals at Ibusuki and Minami Toyota. Very few of the clients there, however, specifically come for Naikan treatment. Rather, they enter the general alcoholism rehabilitation program offered by the facility and first hear about Naikan from their patient peers and therapists.

Each therapist was asked to outline in a few words the special features of his or her facility. Mr. Yoshimoto wrote that the Nara Center is not strictly a religious facility. The implicit comparison here is with the other two established, temple-housed facilities of Gasshoen and Senkobo. The therapists at Gasshoen gave the religious lectures and the presence of the listening Buddha as the key features there. Senkobo therapists considered the strict Zen-like Naikan and the presence of niwazume (those who wait in the temple grounds to be admitted when they have shown their determination and patience—a Zen temple practice) to be the outstanding features of their setting. The therapists at Minami Toyota Hospital and Ibusuki Takemoto Hospital pointed out the use of Naikan in a general program of treatment of alcoholics.

As currently practiced Naikan is, at best, a marginally profitable enterprise, therapists report. Those settings with less concern about financial matters have no problems. Yoshimoto in Nara and his sister-in-law at the Meguro Center are both wealthy from earlier business enterprises. Gasshoen Temple relies on a broad donation base from believers and raises its own food. However, hospitals and Senkobo Temple, with outstanding loans for past construction or heavy operating expenses, find Naikan brings a low return for the time and facilities necessary to the therapy. At all the major Naikan meetings in 1978 there was much talk of increasing fees to cover costs of operation and investment.

Therapists report only minor changes, if any at all, over their few years of Naikan practice. Yoshimoto himself sees no changes in Naikan over forty years except that he has had to add more therapists to handle the increasing number of clients. From an outsider's perspective, it appears to me that there have been significant changes in Naikan over even the past twenty-five years. It has moved from an emphasis on reform of prisoners to a broader clientele. The aura of religion is less strongly attached to the therapy. The therapy has gained some respectability in the academic and psychotherapeutic communities. Its emphasis has moved somewhat from guilt and repentance toward joy and a sense of having been loved. Overall, the therapy has shifted toward accepting a wider perspective and a wider range of presenting problems and motivations among the Naikansha.

Very recent Naikan variations with some reported success (Kusunoki 1980) include a sixty-day period of brief Naikan with a journal record of the recollections turned in to the leader at the end of that time, group Naikan for shorter periods utilizing collective confession and increased amounts of educational material, selective Naikan in which only one of the three themes (e.g., reflecting on what others did for the client) is used for recollection, and Naikan combined with other therapies such as autogenic training, yoga, medication, and specialized diets.

Few of the older Naikan therapists use any treatment form but Naikan. Usami at Senkobo is one exception, using zazen along with Naikan. However, most of the newer therapists use Naikan in conjunction with counseling, medication, hypnosis, zazen, or other therapies. They may disagree on the types of client most easily cured and most difficult to cure by Naikan, but generally the therapists agree that motivation and a desire for self-growth are more important than the presenting complaint. Several mentioned clients with family problems and neuroses as those most readily cured by Naikan. Other highly amenable problems include delinquency, neurotic introversion, alcoholism, psychosomatic complaints, and the lesser difficulties of the normal Naikansha who come for self-development. The joy of doing Naikan comes from watching such clients improve, many of the shidosha wrote.

Naikan appears difficult with unmotivated clients, psychotics, those who have personality disorders, those who are depressed over a lost love, overly introverted clients, and certain kinds of neurotics. Some therapists reported that Naikan would absolutely not cure cancer or other physical illnesses, Parkinsonism, schizophrenia, purposelessness in life, or clients with undeveloped egos. Others disagree, and cite cases that appear to have been helped or cured by Naikan. Miki (1967) holds that the effectiveness of Naikan with schizophrenic and depressive patients is still an open question. Yoshimoto, on the other hand, claims successes in treatment of both these disorders. The claims for breadth must compete with the desires for narrowed scope but greater respectability in scientific/psychotherapeutic circles. At this juncture hard data are in very short supply and Yoshimoto himself, with his years of clinical experience, claims to have no real knowledge that would allow him to predict who would be and who would not be helped significantly by Naikan.

The therapists were asked whether they thought Naikan useful for all ages of Westerners and for Westernized Japanese youth. All agreed that both categories of clients would benefit from Naikan. In the case of Westerners, the reasons offered for Naikan's utility were various: "people are people," "satori [enlightenment] is necessary for all humans," "there is a need for everyone to discover themselves; all were cared for by a mother and father [or surrogates]," "all need to recognize they live because of their mother's love," and "the West needs more of the East's introversion and self-reflection." As for modern

Japan's youth, "young people are selfish and overly dependent," "some young people are looking for truth," "learning to take the other's point of view is ideal for young people," "self-development is easier for youth," "the relationship with the mother is especially important," "they need to get rid of the self," "they need a personal life-purpose to make them responsible," "they must recognize the effort and sacrifices of their parents, then they will work harder," "they need to be freed from their misconceptions about 'self'."

When asked what qualities and training make for a good Naikan therapist, most referred to experience doing Naikan, particularly deep Naikan or daily Naikan. Other qualities mentioned were gratitude, emphathy, love, dedication, energy, toughness yet softness, understanding, ability to listen, acceptance, skill at interviewing, and knowledge about psychology and personality.

Most therapists predicted an expanded use of Naikan in their facility and increasing acceptance of the method by the Japanese people. The only note of doubt was sounded regarding the effect of the inevitable death of the aged Yoshimoto Ishin. The founder of Naikan has remained the focal point of allegiance and inspiration for the burgeoning movement. What force will hold the various practitioners together after Yoshimoto's death? Efforts to unify Naikan through a national organization are described elsewhere. Yoshimoto is deeply involved in encouraging development of this stabilizing organization.

Finally, these fifteen shidosha were asked to classify Naikan in one or more of the categories below. The number in parenthesis is the count of therapists who considered Naikan to belong in that category. Most therapists selected more than one category. Naikan is psychotherapy (9), religion (6), mental/spiritual education (*seishinkyoiku*) (6), self-development (8), and other (4). Fewer were willing to commit themselves in writing to an opinion of what Naikan is not. Three considered Naikan to be something outside of religion, one saw it as not psychotherapy, and one as not mental/spiritual education.

Yoshimoto Sensei's attitude was well reflected in his reply. He wrote simply, "Naikan is Naikan."

Overall, there was some degree of agreement among the therapists on the broad applicability of Naikan, its positive future, its satisfactions (the opportunity of seeing clients improve) and its problems (unmotivated clients and finances). Categorizing Naikan, defining ideal qualities in a therapist, and assessing which kinds of complaints were most easily affected and most difficult to influence by Naikan resulted in a greater variety of responses and in outright disagreement among these practitioners. Certainly, the responses were colored by the therapists' personalities, their work-settings, and their varying periods of experience with Naikan. As is the case in Morita psychotherapy, this diversity of opinion may be considered a positive factor that prevents an overly narrow adaptation to a particular cultural period and allows flexibility that continues to provide a functional fit within a changing cultural milieu.

4 _____ Scope, Results, and Criticism

Naikan has been used with remarkable effectiveness in the treatment of sociopaths and alcoholics. In the 1960s studies of prisoners in Hiroshima, Miyazaki, Takamatsu, Tokushima, and elsewhere showed impressive reductions in recidivism rates for those who did Naikan compared with those who did not. The self-selection of those who chose to do Naikan was not accounted for in any of the studies.

In followup studies reviewed by Tada and Miki (1972) 28 percent of responding prisoners at Kyoto Prison thought others should try Naikan, 55 percent thought it useful for themselves, 11 percent considered it once useful but later did not think about it, and only one prisoner described it as boring. Of these Kyoto prisoners some 27 percent continued to do Naikan at least occasionally, seated and facing the wall, another 33 percent continued Naikan at least sometimes, in bed or elsewhere, 8 percent had tried daily Naikan but had stopped, 2 percent never did bunsan (daily) Naikan, and 25 percent reported doing Naikan-like thinking but not formal Naikan. In a number of studies prisoners and prison officials reported improvement in self-control, attitudes toward work, social orientation, family relationships, as well as other benefits from the self-reflection. It is interesting to read that in the United States, too, a self-reflective technique is being tried out in penal facilities. Due to the success of transcendental meditation at California's Folsom Prison officials are encouraging its use in other parts of the state prison system (*Behavior Today* 1979).

As noted elsewhere, Takemoto reports cure rates for alcoholics in the 60 percent range and improvement in over 80 percent of patients treated. Some preliminary results from these patients, reported by Okawa and Takemoto (1978), indicate that blood pressure, pulse rate, tension level, body discomfort, sleep pattern, appetite, and bowel habits all seem to be affected by Naikan; the deeper the level of Naikan, the more pronounced the effects.

Psychological test-evaluations using attitude-change measures, the P-F scale, TAT, Manifest Anxiety Scale, and sentence-completion tests have shown expected results in terms of decreased self-evaluation and increased other-evaluation with corresponding increased self-punitiveness and decreased levels of punitive attitudes toward others. See Miki (1972b) for a summary of studies to that date and the Naikan Gakkai Proceedings thereafter. The studies are flawed in terms of no controls, inadequate controls, and absence of blind ratings.

A followup study of Naikansha from the Nara Center was reported by Yokoyama (1978). In 1976 questionnaires were mailed to the 466 clients who did Naikan in the year 1974. There were 130 returns, a response rate of 27.9 percent. The questions covered a wide range of topics related to the Naikan experience. If the client was uncomfortable during Naikan the discomfort was most likely to occur in the first three days. Distressing features with highest percentage responses included difficulty concentrating (19 percent), guilt over the past (19 percent), feelings of constriction and isolation (18 percent), difficulty remembering (15 percent), and boredom (10 percent). Thirteen percent of the respondents had no reported distress.

After completion of Naikan the most common feelings were love and gratitude (35 percent), relief and tranquility (29 percent), awarenes of one's own faults (23 percent), better ability to take others' points of view (19 percent), and increased self-confidence and desire to work (13 percent). Twenty-three percent of those reporting stated that they continued Naikan on a daily basis; 18 percent reported sometimes doing bunsan or nichijo (daily) Naikan; 58 percent did not continue Naikan after the intensive week of shuchu Naikan. Some 63 percent reported a desire to do intensive Naikan again.

Yokoyama noted that the most negative attitudes toward Naikan were found in the teenage group and among those pressured to do Naikan by teachers or management.

Although some might disagree with these limitations, it would appear that Naikan is not indicated for children (although very young children in the middle years of elementary school and one five-year-old have done it), persons with very low intelligence, psychotics uncontrolled by medication, severely depressed persons, and resistive unmotivated persons.

According to Mr. Yoshimoto, season, climate, and weather have no effect on the depth of Naikan. The client's motivation has much more influence. In recent times psychiatric hospitals and school authorities have increasingly sent clients for Naikan. Such clients are poorly motivated and are often represented among those who fail to complete the week of meditation.

Kusunoki (1976) lists a number of conditions that appear to have been cured during Naikan. Obsessive compulsive neurosis, phobias, dizziness, stiffness, insomnia, anxiety attacks, breathing problems, nausea, stomach trouble, lack of appetite, writer's cramp; even near-sightedness, rheumatism, hernia, hemorrhoids, and high blood pressure. He goes on to clarify Yoshimoto's position on physical illness. Certainly some illnesses are cured by Naikan but others are not. For a physical problem the client should first go to a physician. Particularly helpful are those physicians who also know about the effectiveness of Naikan. Yoshimoto emphasizes that he is not a physician. However, his name and that of the Nara Center are mentioned in several popular books on Eastern medicine.

Certainly, the established medical profession looks with some doubt on reported cures by Naikan of such diseases as hernia, Parkinsonism, epilepsy, schizophrenia, psychotic depression, and manic depression. Psychosomatic disorders cured by Naikan are much more palatable to current scientific taste. That individual cases diagnosed by a physician were cured, at least temporarily, cannot be denied—but the swallowing and the digestion of such facts by the scientific community are different, though related, processes. The reasons for cure of the more difficult cases are still unknown from the perspective of Western science.

Yamamoto (1972) lists some of the criticisms directed at Naikan by some prison administrators. These specific criticisms represent larger issues that extend beyond the confines of the prison system. Naikan is difficult to practice, some hold, requiring an initial large block of time for client and therapist, specialized, quiet facilities, and great motivation to endure. As practiced in Nara, for example, the necessity of such conditions cannot be denied. Only research experience will tell whether simplified variants of Naikan can be as effective. Some argued that Naikan is a religion and therefore inappropriate in prisons, schools, and companies.

We shall examine below the issue of whether Naikan is a religion. That question aside, the appropriateness of a religious practice in secular settings depends upon its voluntary nature, the costs and rewards involved in practicing it, and its usefulness for promoting the ends defined by the secular institution. Some believe that Naikan fosters the occurrence of suicide. Evidence to date indicates that such fears are groundless. Further monitoring is necessary.

The fine results attributed to Naikan may be consequences of other factors, such as self-selection of clients, some critics have observed. Certainly, the effectiveness of any therapy or the elements of any therapy are difficult to ascertain conclusively. Further studies, involving blind and double-blind designs, will be helpful.

Naikan has been attacked for underplaying the role of parents and society in general in contributing to crime and other misdeeds. Certainly Naikan focuses the client's attention on his own contribution to society's problems. He is to see himself as the offender rather than the victim. Perhaps such a one-sided view is necessary to restore the balance in persons who feel put upon, victimized, and powerless in a hostile world. Perhaps the contrasting non-Naikan emphasis on social causality and lack of personal responsibility is simply wrong. Nevertheless, this argument hits at the heart of Naikan. Japanese therapies tend to show little weakness in terms of internal consistency. If they are to be challenged it is probably in the area of the initial assumptions, the "givens" about the world, that the assault must be made. Other challenges such as the pointing to the resistance to self-reflection in the client or to the initial painfulness of the process or to the unfashionableness of it in the modern world or to the current thinness of theory and limited acceptance of the method in the scholarly and professional worlds can be handled comparatively easily in terms of historic caprice, fads, and the apparent utility of the method. Theory will emerge if successes continue and scholarly interest is sustained.

Criticisms leveled at Naikan have not demolished it in any sense. Challenge of assumptions and stricter, critical evaluation of therapeutic results offer the highest probabilities for significant countervoices in the future. As of now, Naikan seems well on its way to further expansion.

Yoshimoto Ishin, founder of Naikan.

Naikan calligraphy by the founder.

Bowing before the *byobu* screen prior to the *mensetsu* interview.

Mr. and Mrs. Yoshimoto relax in the study at the Nara Naikan Kenshujo.

In the early morning Mr. Naga-shima sweeps the entranceway at the Nara Center.

Yoshimoto's assistant sits before the bank of tape recorders used for duplicating Naikan tapes.

At the *zadankai* meeting, clients publicly confess their faults. A tape recording of the meeting may be purchased later.

At Gasshoen Rev. Mizuno lectures in the early morning to Naikansha and to local farm folk, devout believers in Shinshu Buddhism.

This nun is one of the two therapists who conduct the gentle *mensetsu* at Gasshoen. Although there is no television and only one emergency radio on the temple grounds, a motor scooter is convenient for local errands.

The other Gasshoen Naikan guide picks vegetables in the garden of the largely self-supporting temple complex.

Rev. Usami blends cool Zen and warm Shinshu Buddhism practices at his Naikan temple, Senkobo.

Senkobo, in Mie Prefecture, was newly built for efficient conducting of Zen-like Naikan.

A client at Senkobo meditates facing the wall.

This young man waits for days to be admitted to Senkobo. Called *niwazume*, this demonstration of perseverance and commitment is borrowed from Zen.

At the Kibo Club in Tokyo the therapist listens to a *mensetsu* confession.

All photos are by the author.

5 _____ Naikan Theory

It is not just that everyone is bad but that I am bad.

Yoshimoto Ishin

The development of a genuine scientific theory of Naikan has been slow in beginning. Several factors have contributed to this delay. First is the practice orientation of the committed therapists. These practitioners have the experience to evaluate theoretical constructs of Naikan at least on a preliminary level. But their interest lies in reforming human lives, not in theoretical speculation. They have a method that appears to bring benefit to their clients; from their perspective such benefit alone is sufficient. A second factor has been the persistent influence of Jodo Shinshu Buddhism on Naikan. Religion offers an alternate explanatory schema readily understood by most Naikan therapists. To explain a patient's confession as the result of Amida Buddha working in his heart is a simple and satisfactory conception for many practitioners and for many Naikansha. Finally, Naikan's founder, Yoshimoto, has left the development of a scientific theory for Naikan to the experts in medicine and psychology. After all, he has not been trained in the area of scientific thought. Yet with few exceptions these scientific professionals have had only peripheral interest in Naikan and, it would appear, little interest in the task of original scientific theory-building. Naikan theory to date is fragmentary, vague, and inconsistent with other scientific findings.

Two trends, however, point to renewed effort in this area. One trend is the increasing dissatisfaction with the practice of Naikan as it exists today. Problems of economy, space, time, and discontent with the kinds of explanations offered clients plague particularly the younger therapists who would like to give Naikan a serious try. However, any attempts to make substantial changes in this august treatment mode must have some sound theoretical justification and legitimation. Science could provide an authoritative basis for revisions.

A related trend is the disaffection with the religious trappings of Naikan. For many years now Naikan has met resistance in prisons and juvenile detention facilities because it was seen by some to be a religious practice. Similar difficulties are faced by physicians and psychologists who practice Naikan. They must project an image of Naikan as a modern, science-based therapeutic mode in order to attract certain clients and to maintain their reputation in the professional community. Dissatisfaction with the religious emphasis as well as the need to reevaluate elements of Naikan practice currently provide strong impetus for the development of a comprehensive scientific theory of Naikan.

SELF-IMAGE IN NAIKAN

These days the field of pastoral counseling in the West (for that matter, the field of psychotherapy in general) is replete with admonitions to maintain a positive self-image, build one's own self-esteem, love one's self in order to love others; "I'm okay," and so are you. Personally, I have trouble constantly supporting such a grand view of myself. There are times when I do stupid, thoughtless, even cruel deeds. There are times when I am disheartened, self-critical, alienated.

Perhaps such a rosy self-portrait is an unnecessary overreaction to earlier concepts of man's sinfulness. The earlier emphasis on original sin seemed to lead nowhere but to despair. Naikan's philosophy, too, begins with human weakness—not an abstract taken-as-given inherited weakness but the concrete, detailed weaknesses that anyone who reflects on his past is bound to find. And Naikan balances this weakness with the recollection of having been loved and cared for in spite of it. Again, the loving was not offered by some distant, vague God figure but by real people in one's everyday life as one grew up, and the love continues to be given to us as adults. Finally, Naikan juxtaposes the human selfishness and failures that resulted from our weakness with the caring concern of others and suggests that the natural response to recognition of this discrepancy will be gratitude and a desire to serve others. Thus, the realization of one's own unworthiness and imperfection (sinfulness, if you will) leads not to the hell of depression but to a positive thankfulness and life purpose. A fine (inflated) self-image may not be necessary for a meaningful, joyful life. Certainly, it is easier for me to maintain a consistent self-concept when I start at a more self-effacing level. When success occurs I can be grateful to others for their part in producing it for me. When I fail and when the unpleasant, ugly side of my character shows itself, then it is comforting to know that others continue to care for me in concrete ways in spite of the reality of this uneven lifeway of mine. In a sense, a positive self image is a target for the "slings and arrows of outrageous fortune." Presenting to others a social image of skill and competence may invite challenges, sniping, and resentment, as when the neurotic patient dares his analyst to cure him or the student seeks to frame a question his professor cannot answer. A more modest stance may not eliminate such challenges, but it results in a more defensible position, one less likely to summon ego defensiveness in self and others and more likely to permit a supportive, other-oriented response.

The gratitude spreads beyond human relationships to the grateful use of things. Water, air, electricity can be used well, allowing these life elements to fulfill their purposes before "dying." Words of others are "stolen" if not listened to carefully, lovingly. Time is "robbed" when one makes an acquaintance wait because one is late for an appointment. One "owes" one's dishes and chairs and floors for the life support they have provided. One's car can be "repaid" by regular servicing and careful driving. One's own body has offered service worthy of good treatment.

On paper this philosophy is at least internally consistent. Lived out, it appears to make a great deal of sense. It is a viable life philosophy for those who practice Naikan's way.

NAIKAN'S FOUNDATION

The philosophical roots of Naikan lie in Jodo Shinshu Buddhism. Shinshu, particularly since the elaboration by Rennyo (1415–99) of the ideas of the founder, Shinran (1173–1262), held both a faith and an action doctrine. Called the twofold truth *shintai zokutai*, the *shintai* aspect dealt with salvation achieved through calling on Amida's divine power, and the *zokutai* aspect emphasized unselfish works as a member of the social order. This latter, almost Confucian, concern with moral order and virtuous behavior extends into Naikan's emphasis on the practical daily deeds that reflect one's inner condition of gratitude, selflessness, loving.

It was during the interval between Shinran and Rennyo that Ryoyo Shogei (1341–1420) began what I consider the "psychologizing" of Shinshu religion by holding that " 'Rebirth' is a metaphor for the transformation of the psychic processes of the individual within himself. . . . It is a condition of the mind" (Saunders 1964, 240). Even at Gasshoen, where Naikan is conducted in a temple context, religious words such as "heaven," "hell," "devils," and "saints" are defined in terms of current life conditions and states of the heart rather than in mystical, otherworldly terms. And, of course, Naikan itself is the ultimate psychologization of Shinshu faith, a religious practice turned into psychotherapy.

Parallels with modern Christian theology and religious practice are readily apparent. In contemporary liberal Christianity emphasis is placed on this-worldly attitudes and acts, social service ("the social gospel"), and pastoral counseling. In this sense, the psychologized, demythologized, rationalized Naikan version of Shinshu belief would offer little offense to those with a Christian background. On the contrary, a Christian ministry groping about for a technique and a position firmer than the fragile I'm-OK-You're-OK vogue might find in Naikan a method worth serious consideration.

The historical models for Naikan practice lay in the improbable combination of a meditative discipline for monastic life and commercial business accounting. As noted above, mishirabe was a severe meditative practice carried out by priests of one subsect of Jodo Shinshu Buddhism. In isolation, without sleep or food, they sought enlightenment through reflection on their past. Yoshimoto, after several unsuccessful tries, finally attained satori through this means. Subsequently he removed the physical hardships and devised the three themes for self-reflection and the frequent mensetsu interviews, thus reshaping the specialized religious practice into a means for self-growth available to the lay person.

Formerly, Yoshimoto was a businessman, a company president. Periodically it was necessary to balance the books, that is, to compare what had been taken in with what had been produced and sent out. Yoshimoto adapted this bookkeeping process to the whole of social life. In a sense, Naikan can be seen as an evaluation of how much one has borrowed from and loaned to one's significant others, a social ledger, if you will (Yoshimoto 1978).

The practice of Naikan raises some fundamental questions about the moral nature of human beings. The assumption underlying Naikan practice is that we are all moral creatures. That is, we store information about our unbalanced social exchanges, suppress that information (keep it from awareness), and recall it again under proper conditions. The retrieved perceptions of our past behaviors have the attributes of moral evaluation. That is, the past events are not perceived dispassionately. Rather, as they are recalled in the Naikan setting, they are strongly colored by feelings of guilt, gratitude, self-recrimination, repentance, and the like.

The question is, of course, whether the recollections were initially coded and stored with such moral tones or whether the recollection process itself (the Naikan reflection) adds the moral shading to recalled events that were initially coded in amoral form.

There does seem to be some selection in terms of what Naikan clients recalled about the past before and after Naikan. Events and habits that showed the client in a negative light were less often recalled before Naikan. Why should it be that under normal circumstances, we tend to recall our own helpfulness to others and their mistreatment of us? Why do we take for granted what we have received from others and criticize others' lack of appreciation of our efforts in their behalf? If memories were not coded with a moral "soundtrack" one would expect us to recall helping and being helped equally well and frequently. Such does not seem to be the case, however.

The social world probably is not constructed in the clear black-and-white fashion Naikan seems to suggest. But it may very well be a darker shade of gray than we are accustomed to perceive. We are not comfortable recognizing our debts to others and our mistreatment of them. We want to think of ourselves as persons who have at least returned what we have received. Such a self-image distinguishes us from those on welfare rolls, from wards of the state, from chronically hospitalized psychiatric patients, and from others we wish to consider our moral inferiors.

Yet Naikan proposes the discomfiting proposition that we are not so different, after all. We are all the recipients of "grace" from our social (and physical) world. That is, we have indulged in the unmerited favor of those around us, quickly forgetting the large and small deeds afforded us by others, remembering, rather, what we have done for them and the trouble they have caused us.

Naikan slices through this ordinary perception and recollection. Naikan reverses the view of one's social ledger and, in the process, produces profound emotional and motivational changes in many Naikansha.

Takeuchi (1965) sees a connection between Naikan and Frankl's theory in which there are, underlying consciousness, two unconscious worlds—one of self-oriented impulses and one of other-oriented morality. Takeuchi argues that if this basic moral self did not exist Naikansha would not recall their misdeeds in the distant past. *Something* caused them to code and store in memory their acts of stealing, lying, grumbling, and sloth, with the resulting opportunity, through Naikan reflection, of reversing the lifelong balance of power between the self-centered and moral aspects of their unconscious. He holds that the concepts of sin (Frankl's "responsibility") and love are the foundations of morality and religion. Naikan aims at evoking recognition of these two basic elements.

Miki (1978), too, sees these elements as basic to Naikan. He offers an analysis of the five types of sin (the term is unfashionable in some circles these days; perhaps "moral misdeeds" or "proscribed attitudes and behaviors" will be more acceptable to some readers) realized by Naikansha. First is the neglected exchange, the failure to return to others as they have given. Second is the misdeed, the act of commission such as lying and stealing. Third is the sin of omission, what should have been done but was not. (The professor who neglects to provide encouragement and support for needy graduate students, the elder brother who refuses to play with his lonely sister.) Fourth, one finds proper acts that were carried out, but with a poor attitude, that is, they were not "from the heart." The fifth and last category does not involve behavior at all but is that collection of hateful, hurting, and resentful thoughts that rarely find overt expression.

Miki, following basic Naikan theory, points out that the last three (in

89

fact, all five) are related to the inability or unwillingness to view the world from another's point of view, to empathize with one's neighbor. If one could truly stand in another's shoes one would not do him wrong.

This principle is a corollary of the Buddhist tenet that all evil results from ignorance. If one "really" knew the consequences of one's acts one would do only good. Of course, Naikan, emerging from Shinshu Buddhism, aims precisely at having the Naikansha review (re-view) his past from the perspective of significant others in his life. The instructions at mensetsu are not "Haha no koto wo shirabete kudasai" (Examine your mother) but "Haha ni taishite jibun no kotowo shira-bete kudasai" (Examine yourself *in regard to* or being confronted with your mother). The supplemental instructions spell out the goal of viewing yourself as *she saw you*.

THE TRUE SELF

Why, then, do we not all live this Naikan way, recognizing what we truly are and spending our lives trying to begin to repay in some small measure what we owe to our social world? Put in a Naikan way, What causes us to become separated from our true selves? The Naikan theorist points to two main reasons: avoidance and ignorance. There is avoidance because on some level we fear to recognize this social debt. The fearsome vision of the burden we would feel, the guilt we would bear in realizing deeply that we have taken and taken since even before the moment of our birth and have given so little in return causes us to close our eyes to the truth. We learn early to use people, to take from them and to cover up our taking. There is ignorance because realization brings, in the end, not the suffocating guilt that we expect and fear but soaring gratitude and, with it, fresh purpose in life. When we understand who we really are there is no need for external commands to do this or do that; rather, spontaneously, even joyfully we lose ourselves in the service of those around us. If Socrates' admonition to "know thyself" is aimed at discovering the self never before known, Naikan's "know thyself" admonition is to rediscover the self that has become separated (iso-lated) from its original state through misdeeds (Yamamoto, 1972.)

The Naikan therapist holds that it is not sufficient for us to say "Ah yes, you are right. I owe a great debt to the world. I should strive to repay it." To do so would be to engage merely in superficial word play. To gain a genuine sense of the overwhelming nature of what we receive from others, as contrasted with what little we return and what troubles we needlessly cause others, it is necessary to examine our lives in great detail. This deeper understanding of Naikan truths comes through guided Naikan reflection. And that reflection leads to service.

As I noted in the Acknowledgements for this book, from the perspective of this Japanese therapy form it would be narrow-minded and, flatly, incorrect for me to credit *myself* with the writing of the book. The properly examined life will be lived in sacrifice for others, with humility and deep gratitude. What absurd pomposity it would be for me to be prideful of a body and mind nurtured through the efforts of others.

THEORETICAL DEBATE

> "A diamond will never be beautiful—not for thousands of years in its original state—until cut and polished."
>
> Rev. Usami
>
> "A tree must be pruned, grafted."
>
> Rev. Mizuno

Within Naikan theory perhaps the hottest theoretical argument revolves around the negative, painful side of self-reflection. For me, the issue was symbolized by the assigned reflection themes such as lying, stealing, and rule-breaking. Unlike the more common assignments of what was received from, returned to, and what troubles were caused some significant other, in the themes of lying, stealing, and the like (I shall call them sinning themes) there is no possible balance implied either in terms of what was given and what was received or in terms of a balance between gratitude (for having been loved) and guilt (for having failed others). Sinning themes focus solely on the negative side of human existence.

Some theorists hold that recognition of appropriate gratitude (*kansha*) is sufficient to cause life change in Naikan clients. Others argue that the feeling of guilt and the demolishing of an inflated self-image (the humility of *sumanai*) are necessary to achieve desired results. Certainly sinning themes are designed to produce sumanai feelings.

Those who argue against a strong guilt-inducement emphasis point to the dark image Naikan has earned in some circles. The method is readily dismissed at first glance by many (in the East and in the West) because of what appears to be an obsession with sin. The danger of unhealthy effects on the self-concept of some already guiltridden neurotics and the potential danger of suicide are also pointed out. One can give up the self out of gratitude as well as out of remorse, they hold.

While some Naikan professionals are wondering how to deemphasize the factor of guilt produced by Naikan, the Morita therapist would state simply that although guilt is unpleasant (and certainly its unpleasantness is not likely to attract many clients to Naikan), it is nevertheless no worse or no better than any other feeling. It simply is.

Guilt is useful, again like any other feeling. It is to be felt, accepted, examined for information it may provide about what needs to be done; and then attention is to be turned to appropriate behavior, the Moritist would say.

The Naikan therapist hurts, too, in empathizing with the client's discomfort with guilt. The Morita therapist retains more detachment in the face of the inevitability of unpleasant feelings flowing through attention. Both kinds of therapist are concerned with the behavioral changes which follow, but this contrast in attitudes toward feelings illustrates the relative "coolness" of Morita therapy in comparison with Naikan.

The other side of the debate among Naikan practitioners holds both kansha and sumanai to be essential for the major restructuring of a life-view. These therapists distinguish between unhealthy neurotic guilt and realistic existential guilt. If reality has a dark side of neglected responsibility, that must be recognized. And the danger of suicide, they contend, is overblown. In fact, suicides have not occurred more than once or twice among the thousands of Naikansha treated. Existential guilt leads not to suicide but to the desire to sacrifice the self in service. Furthermore, Miki (1978) believes that identification with the therapist helps insulate the client against depression and suicidal potential.

The issue conceivably could be decided experimentally using two forms of Naikan. The debate continues in the realm of words.

RECENT TRENDS

Current concerns in Naikan are reflected in the content of a Naikan planning meeting held in the fall of 1978. In the placid setting of Kiyosumi Gardens, famous for the intricate placement of large rocks gathered from throughout Japan, thirty persons from around the country came together to plan the future of Naikan.

Four major topics arose during discussions at the meeting. The first had to do with pre-Naikan and post-Naikan matters. What sorts of preparations are helpful or necessary in order that the client do intensive Naikan well? Some practitioners used a period of counseling to establish a relation of trust and to allow the client some cathartic outpouring before the structured format of the mensetsu interview began. Another therapist employed hypnosis to weaken resistance and facilitate recollection of past events through hypnotic age regression. Others encouraged attendance at Naikan meetings and played Naikan tapes for prospective clients so that they would know what to expect from Naikan and would have increased motivation to meditate deeply. Methods differed but the consensus seemed to be that some sort of introductory period was helpful.

A related issue dealt with post-Naikan practices. Of course, daily (nichijo) Naikan is the backbone of aftercare. Yet very few clients actually go on to do nichijo Naikan on a daily basis. Post-Naikan group meetings were increasing in number and attendance. The Naikan magazine, postcards, and a newsletter provided followup contact and encouragment. Finally, some Naikan practitioners had begun to specialize in aftercare itself. Such Naikan guides may send their clients to one or another of the Naikan centers for intensive Naikan then pick them up afterward for counseling and support through variations of daily Naikan. Especially in the first year after Naikan, problems of readjustment to daily life lived out through the Naikan way were likely to occur. For example, the family of Naikansha may consider the returned member "strange," overly courteous and overly sensitive to others. Or a businessman may find himself uncomfortable in the competitive world of business negotiation. In such cases, experienced Naikan advisers are helpful.

A second issue concerned the use of auxiliary therapeutic methods during Naikan. To what degree is medication useful for depressed persons and psychotics during Naikan? How can hypnosis be used effectively during meditation? Are counseling, diaries, and letter writing useful adjuncts during Naikan? What degree of physical exercise supports concentration without interfering with the time necessary for immersion in the meditative process? These subissues are by no means resolved; yet they indicate a characteristic willingness to explore alternative supporting measures for the basic Naikan self-reflection.

Third, some concern was expressed concerning the dark, moralistic image of Naikan in both the public and professional therapy worlds. When the emphasis is on recognition of one's own sins rather than on the realization of having been loved and cared for, such an image is readily projected. Terms such as "healthy guilt," "being 'lived' by others," "self-growth," and "self-discovery" have a more positive ring. Those at the meeting agreed that there is a need to emphasize the positive side of Naikan.

Finally, a framework for a national Naikan organization was proposed. Previously, Naikan centers, therapists, and clients were scattered about Japan with only a loose informal tie to Yoshimoto Sensei and his Nara Center. A formal organizational structure was set forth at the planning meeting. Representatives from all of the major areas of Japan (and one international representative) were selected. Care was taken to include each of the Naikan specialty areas: psychology, medicine, education, business, religion, correctional facilities, and the

Naikan centers which seem to fit in none of the other categories. Legal incorporation, at that time, seemed unnecessarily difficult, politically, and expensive. Procedures for elections, membership, dues, and setting up an annual meeting were decided upon.

Subsequently, annual meetings were held in 1979 (Kyoto), 1980 (Okayama), 1981 (Tokyo), and 1982 (Kagoshima). The national organization was ratified and began functioning. The concerns with Naikan preparations and post-Naikan support remained strong during these years. More attention was paid to Naikan styles and alternatives. Increasing interest began to be demonstrated in the practice of Naikan outside of Japan.

6 _____ Larger Theoretical Issues

> A restless feeling of guilt would always be present with him: he would confess and repent and be absolved, confess and repent again and be absolved again, fruitlessly. Perhaps that first hasty confession wrung from him by the fear of hell had not been good? Perhaps, concerned only for his imminent doom, he had not had sincere sorrow for his sin? But the surest sign that his confession had been good and that he had had sincere sorrow for his sin was, he knew, the amendment of his life.
>
> James Joyce, *A Portrait of the Artist as a Young Man*

In this chapter we view some broader concerns raised by a consideration of Naikan. Can this study of a Japanese therapy add to our understanding of what psychotherapy is? How does Naikan compare with other therapies, Eastern and Western? Finally, if we keep Naikan in mind, what can be said about social-science interpretations of social reciprocity and social relations?

CLASSIFICATION

In this section I consider whether Naikan is best classified as a religion, a psychotherapy, an educational method, or some combination of these categories. Such an exercise forces us to look carefully at our definitions of religion, psychotherapy, and education. One of the functions of anthropology is to bring forth the non-Western case in order to challenge and to stretch our Western definitions and hypotheses.

Taking Naikan as a psychotherapy form, the next section concerns its comparison with other therapies from the East and from the West. Finally, in the subsequent section I examine what Naikan suggests are the foundations of human society—the mother-child relationship and reciprocity.

Categorizing is sometimes merely an academic exercise, a kind of intellectual sorting game, an effort to reslice the world-pie. For Naikan, however, being pigeonholed in one category or another has had important practical consequences. If Naikan is religion, many Japanese penal authorities would hold, it does not belong in prisons as part of a rehabilitation program. If Naikan is psychotherapy, some Shinshu believers argue, it does not belong in temples. How can it be reasonably employed in psychiatric hospitals and high schools, in company training programs and religious retreats, in juvenile detention facilities and on daily commuter trains?

Theoretical arguments one way or another have been offered by a number of learned people, often with the apparent purpose of corraling Naikan into their own camp. Kato (1969), director of Japan's National Institute of Mental Health, holds that Naikan is therapy, not religion. He points out that Naikan, like other therapies, permits independent judgment and critical evaluation, allows changes in procedure, allows nonbelievers to practice it, and depends on more than inspiration for its ideological support. Shinfuku (1971), then chairman of the Department of Psychiatry at Jikei University Medical School, found it difficult to differentiate therapy from education; nevertheless he argued that Naikan, while containing educational elements, is therapy. Working primarily with persons suffering from abnormal conditions, Naikan therapists would improve their success through careful psychiatric diagnosis of potential clients, Shinfuku believed.

Yoshimoto himself, in *Naikan Therapy* (1972), argued that a treatment form that does not conflict with other religions, offers no salvation, has no church or scriptures, and requires no sermons cannot be a religion. He found it hard to classify Naikan at all.

Yet Kusunoki (1978), Usami, Mizuno, and others point to the historical and philosophical roots of Naikan. The practice undeniably emerged from Jodo Shinshu Buddhism. For most of its existence Naikan was associated, in the press and in the public mind, with religion. And what is called today the Naikan Training Center (Naikan Kenshujo) in Nara was called the Naikan Educational Training Center in 1971 and simply the Naikan Temple twenty years ago. One cannot easily shake off such a religious association.

One contribution to this discussion would be an examination of the categories themselves—education, religion, and therapy—before assigning Naikan to one or the other of them. A few words of background for this examination are in order.

Much human activity is directed ultimately toward helping the actor achieve a greater sense of control over the world, including some influence over other humans who populate the immediate social world. On the macrolevel, in Adler's theorizing, and on the microlevel, in Soskin and John's (1963) paradigm for analysis of brief speech episodes, the thrust of some human energy toward having a sense of being in control of the immediate situation is apparent. Obtaining information and organizing and reorganizing data are important correlates of this need to feel in control. One needs an orderly sense of what is happening in order to act effectively. Exploration of the environment (information-seeking) (e.g., head-turning and grasping) and efforts to control it (e.g., through crying) are noticeable in humans from infancy. The type of information sought, the hierarchies of organization, and the particular strategies for influencing other persons develop more sophistication with age, usually, but the efforts to avoid impotence do not disappear.

One of the primary purposes of education is the transmission of information or ways of organizing information. In this sense it follows that psychotherapy can be classified as a kind of education—specialized education, to be sure (London 1964; Shinfuku 1971), but certainly a way of helping the client structure the understanding of experience.

What ordinarily brings a neurotic patient to a therapist is some form of suffering. But, as Buddhists have long pointed out, suffering is part of the human condition for all of us. No therapist can totally remove a patient's hurting, sorrow, anger, shyness, inferiority feelings, fear, or grief. Freud remarked in similar fashion that what psychoanalysis could offer the patient was to turn neurotic misery into ordinary human suffering. The therapist cannot absolutely relieve unpleasant feelings in herself/himself, even. What therapy offers is information and a way of reorganizing what the patient already knows or learns during therapy in order to increase that sense of control over the world. When the patient has a vocabulary to define suffering, a model for understanding its source, and a plan for dealing with it, there is more of a sense of having a handle on life. Of course, the vocabularies, models, and plans differ from therapy to therapy, but the overall goals and methods of shamans and psychotherapists, Eastern and Western, are similar on this level of abstraction. A by-product of this specialized educational process should be reduced suffering, at least that suffering which resulted from (or was) feelings of helplessness in dealing with symptoms. And, sometimes other symptoms are relieved, as well.

Here is an intellectual puzzle: Naikan is claimed by some to be a psychotherapy, yet Naikan therapists actually increase the client's discomfort and guilt within the process of treatment. A parallel case from Japan is that of the Morita therapists, who claim to be disinterested in helping the client to feel better at all; rather they teach the client to respond appropriately, regardless of feelings, to what reality brings in each moment. The problem here is that we confront two "psychotherapies" that do not aim at symptom reduction. Naikan aims at reviewing the self in the past and Morita therapy aims at constructive behavior in the present. Whatever "improvements" may occur in the client's discomfort are seen as secondary, even trivial, compared with the primary goals.

So if our definition of psychotherapy is to encompass these Japanese treatment modes, the definition must include a therapeutic goal broader than relieved feelings. On the other hand, I have yet to meet a psychotherapy client in Japan or in the United States whose primary goal was anything other than "feeling better" about himself/herself, the job, the marriage, and the like, or relieving feelings of shyness, fears, anxieties, and so forth.

London (1964) writes that "[The psychotherapist's] purpose is to alleviate the suffering, the mental anguish, the anxiety, the guilt, the neurosis or psychosis of the client" (p. 4). He goes on to argue that in order to do so the psychotherapist must implicitly or explicitly hold and teach a moral, ideological system. London is right, it would appear, but he may not have gone far enough in his argument. It would seem from these Japanese psychotherapeutic systems that the teaching can occur without the primary purpose of alleviating the suffering.

One way of looking at the difference between other forms of education and psychotherapy is that in psychotherapy there is a specific goal of using the transmitted information to increase the client's lost or diminished sense of control over his/her phenomenological world, including the symptoms. From this perspective, if the staff members of a psychiatric ward in a hospital foster a sense of impotence in the patients treated there (Reynolds and Farberow, 1976), they are not practicing psychotherapy but rather custodial care.

To restate this conceptualization of psychotherapy: persons ordinarily come for treatment because they are suffering or are dissatisfied in some way. The suffering may be the discomfort of a phobia, anxiety, feelings of worthlessness, depression, lack of confidence, a distressing life-situation, and the like. Cure involves identifying the problem and instructing the client in such a way as to result in an increased sense of mastery or control over the distressing phenomenological state. These two elements of instruction and mastery seem to be present in all curing. They represent general human goals of organizing data input and having a sense of control over life circumstances.

Let us continue our analysis of psychotherapy in terms of these two elements. When appearing for treatment the suffering client already has some framework for understanding the problem. That is, the client has words that can be used to describe what seems to be bothersome. "I am depressed all of the time." "My head hurts." "I'm nervous." "I hate my father-in-law." These utterances are examples of such organized descriptions, though the range varies considerably in degree of vagueness. Even those who appear at first blush to possess no such framework, on closer examination turn out to fit the model after all. For example, schizophrenic or manic patients brought to the hospital or clinic against their will by family members may define their problem in terms of difficulties with their families: "They don't listen to me when I say that I am fine," or "They take me places to which I don't want to go [e.g., the hospital]," and so forth.

The patient's schema for organizing an interpretation of the problem may or may not correspond (in varying degrees) to that of the therapist. The two frameworks never correspond exactly. There must be an educational element in the therapy by which the therapist transmits some of his/her understanding of the situated problem to the patient (London 1964). And that psychotherapeutic understanding, either directly or through subsequent action, is designed to give the patient an improved way of dealing with the presenting problem.

Better control doesn't necessarily mean elimination of the problem, as we have seen from the cases of Naikan and Morita therapy. Cure doesn't necessarily mean doing away with the presenting complaint. But it always involves reduction of the "dis-order", the sense of being overwhelmed by the phenomenal circumstances. Thus, my proposed definition of psychotherapy must include "an educational process designed to give the client an increased sense of control over experienced living."

In some Western therapies the sense of mastery is usually evoked through increased rational understanding. Be it an "insight" therapy or a token reinforcement program of behavior therapy, the increased sense of control comes from learning paradigms for explaining and discovering how symptoms originate and how one deals with them systematically. This understanding is typically personalized and "taught" through the important interactions between client and therapist (Frank 1961; Freud 1933). Other therapies may offer control through teaching the client to turn himself/herself over to the therapists (be they priests, psychologists, or shamans) who govern the evil spirits or totemic powers in the problem area through some form of acceptance of the problems as they are, through appeal to a divine intervenor, or through various other means.

Again, it must be emphasized that although symptom elimination need not be the goal (even in Western therapies) increased mastery or influence over the discomfort is always sought. The latter is almost always possible to achieve, the former is sometimes very difficult or impossible. Client satisfaction depends, it appears, on the sense of increased control and not on symptom elimination, though sometimes the two are related.

Perhaps it would be helpful to remind the reader here that definitions are neither right nor wrong, they are either more or less useful for given purposes. Let us carry these definitions a bit further before deciding on their usefulness.

One function of some religions appears to be similar to that of psychotherapy. If therapy is a form of education aimed at personalized instruction and an increased sense of control over the experienced world, religion often extends that sense of mastery or potency through loss of the self or giving up of the self. Shamans, faith healers, and Zen priests may utilize the elements of loss of self and the abandonment of self as parts of their educational processes. Psychological cure may occur by religious means as well as by psychotherapeutic means. Certainly, the organization of new information and the reorganization of previously acquired information (i.e., education) occurs in religious as well as psychotherapeutic contexts. The key differentiating factor may be in the purposeful erasure, however temporary, of the conscious ego within the religious context.

By the loss and giving up of the self the whole basic human need to have a sense of mastery over experienced circumstance seems to be transcended. Difficulties are perceived from a radically different perspective or they fade from attention altogether. The Christian may become lost in prayer and meditation, the shaman in trance or possession, the Zen monk in focused attention, the Naikansha in reflection on the past.

From these considerations it seems that Naikan functions as religion, psychotherapy, and education. Kusunoki (1978) writes that with deep reflection comes recognition of one's bad self; then follows giving up on the self, dependence on the Buddha, and a new confidence. Prison Naikansha commonly report a sense of helplessness, of having struggled to conquer life on their own, and of realizing that they have failed. Turning their lives over to the Buddha is, in a sense, a way of expressing the experience of relinquishing the need to feel in control of one's experienced circumstances, including one's suffering. This turning over one's experienced world to others, or to the Buddha or Fate, is sometimes followed by a tremendous sense of relief and joy.

Perhaps an important source of that relief is the recognition that one can turn over control of one's life to another power and still survive. It is not uncommon to hear such an insight verbalized at an Alcoholics Anonymous meeting in the United States. The client does not seem to need to understand fully what is happening. Even much of the information-processing function can be submitted to the other power(s). The focus on the self, with its search for information and mastery over symptoms, is considerably reduced.

Thus, according to the classification system outlined above, Naikan functions as religion, psychotherapy, and education. So the issue of the presence of a religious practice in prisons, schools, hospitals, and businesses must be faced squarely in Japan. The complications are many, but the primary consideration appears to be the degree to which participation in Naikan within these settings is voluntary, without external coercion or auxiliary rewards. The moral, ethical, and legal aspects of this issue are beyond the author's competence and the scope of this book.

NAIKAN AND RECIPROCITY

> Relation is reciprocity. My you acts on me as I act on it. Our students teach us, our works form us . . . we live in the currents of universal reciprocity.
>
> Martin Buber, *I and Thou*

We consider here whether Naikan theory has the potential for contributing to Western social-science theory. Reciprocity and social exchange have been useful concepts in understanding human behavior. Gouldner (1960) used the idea of reciprocity to shore functionalist theory by avoiding the characteristic circular arguments of early functionalism and by admitting apparently dysfunctional, nonreciprocal elements based on inequality of power into the study of society. Gouldner distinguished three meanings for the term "reciprocity": (1) the actual exchange of contingent behaviors, (2) the folk understandings regarding such exchanges, and (3) a moral norm about reciprocity in general. The distinction between 2 and 3 lies in the difference between exchanges based on the relative social positions of the actors and exchanges based on what they have actually done for each other in the past. Of course, one could argue that 3 is a subset of 2 in that such a norm is related to a broad social category like "culture member" or "human." Gouldner specifically eschewed such a position, though his reasons for doing so are not clear to me.

It is precisely in this area of difference between reciprocity on the basis of social role and reciprocity on the basis of general moral norm that Naikan is operating. One can expect services to be performed by one's mother because they are an expected part of her role. And socially, one may not be expected to repay her, as a child, for her services. However, in the general moral norm, she is a person who has given, and she deserves recompense from the person who has received. Gouldner, analyzing the broad moral norm, sees two interrelated components: "(1) people should help those who have helped them, and (2) people should not injure those who have helped them" (p. 171). The three themes of Naikan self-reflection neatly fit within this scheme. "What was received" identifies the helper; "what was returned" examines the degree of compliance with the requirement of helping those who have helped us; and "What troubles were caused" brings to light the ways in which the Naikansha hurt those who helped him.

Gouldner goes on to list some of the criteria by which the moral debt may be measured, for example, the degree of need in the recipient, the amount of sacrifice involved for the donor, the donor's motives, and the voluntary nature of the donation. One might add to Gouldner's list the span of time involved, the resistiveness of the recipient, and the attitude of the donor in giving. If this norm of reciprocity, with these corollary criteria for measuring the debt, is universal, as both Gouldner and Yoshimoto hold, it appears that Naikan is tapping something broader than narrow Japanese cultural norms, something panhuman.

Thus, Gouldner's theory has contributed a broadened sociological base for Naikan. Can Naikan theory add something to Gouldner's formulation? Let us ask what would follow from the Naikan assumption that, in addition to this moral norm, there is recognition that everyone fails to meet it. Awareness of the reality that under normal circumstances one cannot ever repay one's parents, *will* not repay them, might underlie feelings of shyness, stage fright, inferiority. In other words, standing before society (either literally or in imagination), one recognizes at some level one's default on this norm. The self-image "I am a moral, responsible person" can be sustained only at the cost of lying to oneself and to others. Thus, the norm of reciprocity inevitably carries with it a corollary of failure.

Working on a lower level of abstraction, Homans (1961) considered social exchanges as the elementary building blocks of social relations and, ultimately, of societies. Homans argues that each person seeks maximal profit (i.e., maximum rewards at minimal cost) in the exchanges of materials and services (including, for example, signals of esteem and approval). From this narrower view (compared with Gouldner's) one *gives* only because of some anticipated reinforcer from the recipient of the donation. A generalized norm of reciprocity is unnecessary from Homans's perspective. A dynamic equilibrium of exchange will always be achieved in a stable relationship. Although such conditions may obtain in the short run in some social interactions, they do not seem to be present in, say, a parent-infant interaction unless one does some elaborate contortions in interpreting the elements of the system. What does an infant have to offer that is equivalent to the gift of life, feeding, bathing, and so forth? And there appears to be no sense of perceived injustice by parents in this unbalanced exchange. We humans begin our lives with an extended period of extreme dependency. That is a fact. No simple exchange or reciprocity theory can account for interactions during that period without concluding that parents, in general, participate in a long-term unbalanced exchange.

The most parsimonious theoretical addition which allows a reasonable explanation of this reality of unbalanced exchange is a transferral clause. That is, we can pass on to others (usually our children) in goods and services what we have received from our parents. An alternative, the delay clause, involving repayment of one's debt to one's parents when they are old, has commonly been evoked but has difficulty generating equivalencies for life itself, for teaching of basic social and survival skills, and so forth. Homans's theory requires a lot of patching to fit observable reality.

Interestingly, these two Western theories of social interaction have resulted in views involving, on the one hand, self-centered striving for maximal profit (Homans), and, on the other hand, social balancing of reciprocal moral obligations (Gouldner). And the latter theory seems to cover more of the "social territory" than the former.

Folk understandings and scholarly interpretations of Japanese culture have given much attention to the exchange elements described above. Befu (1974) considers gift-giving as a changing custom in modernizing Japan. His categories of gift-giving are rather artificial in that he sees (1) the value of the gift to be unimportant in personal gift-giving, and (2) gift-giving to obtain desired ends as a special category of socially acceptable bribery. In fact, the value of a gift must be considered in all types of gift exchanges in Japan, whether they be obligation-based or personal in nature, and influencing others by giving permeates every sort of gift-giving category Befu offers.

Lebra (1974) looks at the reciprocity principle as it is worked out in the Japanese concept of *on*, a social debt. Lebra points out the difficulty of assessing equivalencies in social exchanges. Sometimes it appears that the reciprocity is not symmetrical at all.

The Japanese case that she offers illustrates Gouldner's point that status and its associated power can maintain equilibrium in an unbalanced exchange. For example, the person in power can choose whether to grant a favor. But, once received, the favor *must* be repayed. And, as Lebra points out, the Japanese person, from childhood, "is reminded of the fathomless *on* he owes to his parents, ancestors, country and countless fellow human beings, alive and deceased, known and unknown to him, for his life, and for what he is today." (p. 195).

Certainly, there cannot be direct reciprocity in these relationships. The debts incurred, in some cases from the moment of birth, cannot be repaid to benefactors who are no longer living, who are not known personally by the recipient, or who comprise a large body such as all members of the country. As we have seen, Naikan focuses attention on those we could make efforts to repay but usually do not. But those who do Naikan deeply for long periods begin to look for ways of repaying ancestors, the country, even inanimate objects and energies like food and electricity. What have you done lately for water, or your pen, or your reading chair? The questions are not ridiculous, given the Naikan perspective on reciprocity.

NAIKAN AND THE ARCHITECTURE OF SOCIAL RELATIONS

I have presented elsewhere (Reynolds 1977) the case for viewing Naikan as resocialization. Briefly, because we cannot actually relive and thus change childhood experiences, it is only possible to reevaluate them, to review them from another perspective. Naikan regresses the client through memory and imagination. And just as if Yoshimoto had read George Herbert Mead (though he has not), the beginning client is persuaded to take on the point of view of significant others in considering himself as a child. Of course, Mead (1913) suggested that this is the very way all humans develop an idea of self in early childhood. We perceive others perceiving us. Thus, Yoshimoto seems to have hit upon a way *to create a new self* through guided imagery.

It is also interesting that, coming from a completely different starting point, Yoshimoto arrived at the conclusion that the mother-child relationship is the prototype and basis for all human social relations. This same conclusion was reached by Freud and Rank and may be supported by ethological observations of other species, as well. Certainly, experimental work with primates indicates that distortions in mothering result in offspring who as adults are unable to engage in the range of appropriate social behaviors. Through the Naikan lens, however, it is the *adequate* mother who allows us to limit ourselves, as we take her services for granted, and then we apply that same self-centered ingratitude toward others in our social world.

DeVos (1980) has rightly pointed out that the Christian tradition directed the individual's supreme love and gratitude toward the sacrificial Christ, thus providing "psychological leverage against . . . the absolute family." The result of this emphasis was that the processes of maturation and of psychotherapy could occur divorced from the familial focus, unlike in Naikan.

Yet the Christian tradition in America continues to promote strong family ties ("The family that prays together, stays together") as well as such values as honor for parents, caring and warm relationships among family members, and acceptance of the individuality of family members.

When I asked Mr. Yoshimoto about doing Naikan on the theme of what Christ had done for the Naikansha, what the client had returned to Christ, and the troubles caused the Diety, Yoshimoto replied that he did not think it appropriate. After all, what can one hope to return to the Cause that has given one everything? There is no conceivable way to balance that debt. More simply, more concretely, how has one kept balanced one's everyday debts with other imperfect creatures such as other humans? The latter investigation seems more practical and urgent from the Naikan founder's point of view.

NAIKAN COMPARED—THE WEST

It is quite proper that you should feel terrible in finding your faults.

Yoshimoto Ishin

If you do anything you please, you are just like animals.

Yoshimoto Ishin

A number of therapies in the East and in the West hold that in order to understand who we are now we must look at who we have been in the past. The content and style of the review of the past vary in the West from, for example, behavior therapy's concern with baseline levels of behaviors and reinforcers, to psychoanalytic exploration of early traumas and relationships. Of course, Naikan also offers the opportunity for reexamination of the client's past.

A number of Japanese authors (Yamamoto 1972a; Takeuchi 1972; Miki 1978; Murase, 1974) have drawn comparisons between Naikan and Western therapies, particularly psychoanalytic ones. Usually the intent of such articles appears to be to bring to light significant similarities and differences in therapies. Occasionally, one finds a paper that seems to aim at justifying Naikan practice by citing Western precedent and theoretical support.

Distinctions between Naikan and Western psychodynamic methods include the following: self-reflection on the past is more guided in Naikan than in free association, reflection on the *recent* past also has value in Naikan, the standpoint from which one is to review these experiences differs (i.e., one tries to take the perspective of the significant other in Naikan), there is a spiritual element to Naikan, the shidosha works exclusively with conscious awareness, more emphasis is on intellectual understanding in the analytic therapies, and more attention is paid to the therapist-patient relationship (e.g., transference) and unconscious resistance in these Western theories of cure. The directive stance of the therapist and minimal focus on the therapist-patient relationship are among the factors that clearly differentiate Rogerian and Naikan therapies. Some have argued that Naikan differs in being a short-term therapy with little therapist contact at all. But Miki (1978) points out that, although contact between therapist and patient is somewhat abridged in Naikan in comparison with the time allowed in Freudian or Rogerian therapies, nevertheless, with an average of three to five minutes per interview and eight to ten interviews per day, this contact time grows to four or even five hours during the course of a week. Furthermore, the therapist's influence goes beyond the direct contact moments and continues over a period in which other interpersonal relationships are disallowed except in private recollection. So the effect of the therapist-patient interaction may be magnified in the absence of these other contacts.

I would add that the fundamental goals of Western therapies and Naikan (along with some other Eastern therapies such as Morita's treatment method) differ. Often Western therapies explicitly aim (quite reasonably and straightforwardly) at reducing symptoms. The basic purpose of Naikan is said to be helping the client discover his "true self." Once he has this new perspective on himself, his symptoms are likely to be eased. But symptom reduction is seen to be only a by-product of Naikan treatment.

Western professionals who have looked at Naikan, albeit briefly and superficially in most cases, have emphasized its potential for inducing guilt, allowing catharsis, and developing superego functions in sociopaths. In other words, the theoretical lenses through which these therapists and scholars viewed Naikan caused the elements of guilt, catharsis, and conscience to stand out in their analyses. They are quick to theorize about Naikan (as their therapies are quick to theorize about patients' problems) using conjecture, imagination, and rational deductive logic to come up with personally satisfying categorical explanations for Naikan's method and effectiveness. The Naikan theorists, on the other hand, are more modest (or timid, depending on one's point of view) in attempting to explain the method in scientific terms. These practitioners tend to stick close to what they understand experientially and to make strong admonitions to the patients on the basis of what they "know" in this sense.

But comparisons with the range of psychoanalytic therapies may not be the most fruitful ones. The strong existential and self-disclosive elements of Naikan may not be best understood within a Freudian framework. For although Naikan practice has elements that are uniquely Japanese, the theory has aspects in common with Western therapy styles characterized by such names as O. H. Mowrer, Sidney Jourard (both psychologists), and Anton Boisen (a minister). These author-therapists present a view of neurosis and cure antithetical to the Freudian psychoanalytic tradition. They do not consider neurosis to be the result of repressed thoughts and suppressed desires; they do not perceive neurotics to be dominated by an overly active superego or conscience. Rather their writings share the theme that the neurotic person has acted in ways that are socially unacceptable (to others and to himself). And rather than reveal this negative aspect of himself to others the neurotic conceals it, with a resultant feeling of alienation from himself and from others.

"They are those who accept the primary loyalties but have failed to measure up to the standards which they feel to be required of them. They are the well-meaning and they want to do right but they stand condemned in their own eyes. There is that in their lives which they are afraid to tell for fear of condemnation. They have not been able to pay the price of growth by renouncing desires and tendencies which belong to an earlier stage of development" (Boisen 1936, p. 201).

Does not that description fit all of us to some degree, in some moments and relationships?

As Jourard (1964) has put it:

> Every maladjusted person is a person who has not made himself known to another human being, and in consequence does not know himself. Nor can he be himself. More than that, *he struggles actively to avoid becoming known by another human being*. He *works* at it ceaselessly . . . .
>
> If I am struggling to avoid becoming known by other persons then, of course, I must construct a false public self. The greater the discrepancy between my unexpurgated real self and the version of myself that I present to others, then the more dangerous will other people be for me. If becoming known by another person is threatening, then the very presence of another person can serve as a stimulus to evoke anxiety, heightened muscle tension, and all the assorted visceral changes which occur when a person is under stress.
>
> When a man does not acknowledge to himself who, what and how he is, he is out of touch with reality, and he will sicken and die and no one can help him without access to the facts. And it seems to be another empirical fact that *no man can acknowledge his real self to himself (that is, know himself) except as an outcome of disclosing himself to another person. . . .*
>
> It is because of the pains arising from real self-being that most of us hide our real selves, even from loved ones, behind the mask of our roles, behind the camouflage of our personage, our public self-being. The price we pay for safety from the penalties of being and being known is steep. It includes loneliness, it includes growing self-alienation, or loss of contact and awareness of our real selves; it includes proneness to mental and physical disease. It includes emptiness and meaninglessness in existence (in Mowrer 1964, pp. 229–30; emphasis in original).

Mowrer is perhaps the most outspoken advocate of this position. He sees symptoms as an *"involuntary confession"* (1964, p. 139), a compromise between public confession and self-protection. It is healthy in that it means the suffering individual is not a sociopath, he cannot break social rules without some pangs of conscience. It is unhealthy in that the neurotic person follows the cowardly line of lies and self-concealment. "A neurosis, it seems, is nothing but a state of guilt that has been neither admitted nor atoned for, and the notion that a person needs some special kind of professional treatment to deliver him from such a condition is surely one of the great illusions of modern times" (Mowrer 1964, p. 225).

If we push Mowrer's argument to an extreme, we can say that all of us have unconfessed wrongs in our life histories, unpalatable acts that we have concealed from others for so long that we have begun to conceal them from ourselves. Recalling and confessing such past wrongs should release energy in the neurotic and the healthy person alike. In another direction, we can say that it is not only a question of wrongs we have done directly to others but also one of what we have taken from others without adequate gratitude and without genuine, systematic attempts to repay them. These acts, attitudes, and failures to respond, too, weigh upon our conscience. Such past experiences should also be recalled and confessed and repaired, when possible. That process is precisely Naikan's concern.

> Once more we are coming to perceive man as preeminently a *social* creature, whose greatest and most devastating anguish is experienced, not in physical pain or biological deprivation, but when he feels alienated, disgraced, guilty, debased—*as a person*. And the thrust of much current therapeutic effort is in the direction of trying to help such individuals recover their social relatedness, community, identity (Mowrer 1964, p. 12; emphasis in original).
>
> Both [psychoanalysis and Mowrer's therapy form] agree that neurosis involves a *moral struggle*; but one holds that this struggle is spurious and wasteful and thus to be "analyzed" away, whereas the other holds that the struggle is valid and worthwhile and, if properly understood and responded to, capable of leading to better things (Mowrer 1964, p. 227; emphasis in original).

Elsewhere (Reynolds 1972) I have written about the similarities among even diverse Western psychotherapies, such as Freudian psychoanalysis and behavior therapy, in the denial of personal responsibility in human behavior, particularly that behavior involved in becoming neurotic and achieving relief from neurosis.

What is the cause of the initial misdeeds which are hidden from others and result in alienation? Mowrer, like the Buddhists, sees the source of "sin" in a healthy drive for success misdirected through unhealthy ignorance.

Let us suppose, for sake of a simple illustration, that there is a *rule* which says that human beings, in going from A to C, ought to do so by moving along the two perpendicular sides of a right-angle triangle, ABC. But "intelligent" people can see that there is a quicker, easier way to make this trip, namely to proceed *directly* from A to C, along the hypotenuse of the triangle. Like misconduct or "sin" in general, this is a short-cut and not, in and of itself, a bad idea. But it so happens that there are certain undesirable later consequences (or "side effects") for persons who go directly from A to C which do not arise if they proceed from A to B to C. Thus ABC becomes the socially approved, moral way to behave and AC is the immoral, disapproved way.

Why do we human beings sometimes, then, act immorally, sinfully? Not because we are necessarily stupid or inherently evil, but because we are personally inexperienced and unwilling to "take the word" of others. I do not believe in Original Sin in the formal theological sense; but I do believe that man is originally a sinner, in the sense that by their very nature rules invite violation, and everyone has to do a certain amount of rule-violating before he "grows up" enough to see the "wisdom of the ages" (Mowrer 1964, p. 228; emphasis in original).

Although there is certainly some truth in what Mowrer has to say on this matter, it is also quite clear that some social rules no longer (if they ever did) point to the wisest, best, most human course of action. Rule violation is one way by which rules come to be changed. The key element missing from Mowrer's argument seems to be that the reasons for each social rule need to be explicit with outcomes described in probabilistic terms. Perhaps in practice such explication is not feasible. But without such a check on the ongoing social system, Mowrer's position amounts to little more than a justification for unthinking conservatism.

Nevertheless, the misdeed is what begins the separation of ourselves from our "true selves," in Naikan terms. There is agreement on the outlines of the source of the human problem. "In this frame of reference, what then is 'therapy'? In essence, it consists of anything which anyone can do to help persuade an estranged, 'neurotic' person (1) to voluntarily confess his mistakes, so that conscience does not have to force the truth out of him 'symptomatically' and (2) to enter into a life of willing sacrifice . . . " (Mowrer 1964, p. 140).

In the West, for about the first four hundred years of Christianity, confession was made in public. Penance was equally a public matter. From the fifth century on the Church began to "seal" confession, making it a private matter between believer and priest. Then, with the Reformation, came the notion that confession need only be made to God, directly, with no priestly intermediary. Mowrer, of course, deplores such a trend.

In Naikan, as we have seen, the initial confession and vow of restitution are made to the therapist within a relatively private setting. Later, however, various group meetings provide the opportunity for public confession. There is abundant literature dealing with the effectiveness of a public commitment in producing and sustaining attitude and behavior change (e.g., Festinger 1964.)

Looked at from this perspective, Naikan practice makes a great deal of sense. The client recognizes his past wrongs, confesses them to the shidosha, then to the assembled Naikansha at the end of the week, then to his family on his return home. He discloses the hidden, negative side of himself and vows to live a life of service to others.

> Therapy, incidentally, may now be defined as the act of helping another individual to make his "conversion," this change-over or transition, from compulsive, "neurotic," conscience-inflicted suffering to the deliberate, voluntary service, cooperation, and loyalty which are the hallmarks of norm-ality. As long as an individual is defiant and unrepentant, his conscience continues to "hurt" him. When he comes to terms with conscience, and with the external community which it represents, the hurting stops and life's zest and meaning return" (Mowrer 1964, p. 241).

The following statement by a patient is from Mowrer (1964). But it could have been written appropriately by a Naikansha. " 'I had hated myself for such a long time that I expected everyone else to hate me, too. And if for some obscure reason they didn't already hate me, they *would* if they knew what I had done. But these two continued to be good to me even after I told them my story. After that I picked out different people to talk to, and continued to be amazed at how they reacted' " (p. 112; emphasis in original).

Both Naikan and these Western therapists have concluded that confession alone is insufficient; service is required also. Kusunoki (1976, p. 246) wrote that one could call the service rendered at places like Gasshoen Temple "work therapy." But the two things are *different*. And the result of sterilizing "service" into "work therapy" has been a movement away from the initial purpose of losing the self in sacrificial effort for others to a sort of meaningless shuffling around to complete artificial, empty tasks. The ultimate in work therapy, perhaps, may be found at one Japanese university hospital inpatient ward where for years some patients have been assigned the task of digging huge pits and then filling them in again. But what alternative is there in a large university hospital with a custodial staff, crowded, technically sophisticated facilities, and busy personnel?

NAIKAN COMPARED—THE EAST

Many psychotherapies in Japan (and other, nontherapeutic enterprises as well) have a familylike structure and a resocialization theme. Naikan is no exception. Other common features include experiential guidance by an authority figure, meditative style, Buddhist-based philosophy, deemphasis of intellectual-rational knowledge, phenomenological focus, immersion in a group in tandem with isolation, the goal of symptom transcendence rather than symptom removal, key experiences reported on the fourth or fifth day of treatment, and humanistic enforcement of severe rules—all these are characteristic of many forms of Japanese psychotherapy. (Reynolds and Yamamoto 1973; Reynolds 1980).

Only one other Japanese therapy form has received the attention of the West as has Naikan. That therapy is Morita's. Although Morita's method was described briefly above, a few words might be usefully offered further comparing Naikan and Morita therapies. Both emerged from Buddhism in a Japanese cultural context. Kodani (1969) saw similarities in the character-education aspects of both, the emphasis on self-disclosure and effort of will, and the minimal reliance on intellectual knowledge. He considered both to stress humility and gratitude, proper attitudes toward life, and both to point out the discrepancy between subjective ideals and imperfect reality. As he put it (p. 43): "A mountain is a mountain. A road doesn't change over the years, but our hearts change and limit us."

Morita therapy is a lifeway and a treatment mode primarily for neurosis and self-growth in normal persons. It aims at having the client accept his feelings as they are, without struggling against them. At the same time the patient is to act in such a way as to accomplish what needs to be done in a given moment. Behavior is controllable directly by the will, feelings are not. If the client attends fully to what he is doing in response to the circumstances reality has placed before him, he will not be troubled by his feelings. Feelings will continue to well up; he will notice them, but his attention will return to the work or conversation or resting or tennis game at hand (Reynolds 1976, 1980).

Murase and Johnson (1973), considering these two therapies, noted the directiveness and authority of the therapist in both but within a predetermined, limited-time framework. Furthermore, both therapies

operate to confirm existing social norms and culturally accepted for-
mulas for living. Both Naikan and Morita therapies emphasize action
more than analytic intellectual understanding, and, in fact, see com-
prehension resulting more from action than from intellectualizing
thought or verbal teaching. Finally, the authors believed that transference and resistance in the Japanese therapies take simplified, stereotypical forms and are not explored directly during therapy as they are
in the West.

As noted above, the two therapies grew from Buddhist notions
about misdirected effort, the consequence of ignorance. The neurotic,
suffering person has the potential for an even better than normal life
once his improper, inefficient suffering-producing attitudes and behaviors are properly channeled. With proper character training
through Naikan or Morita therapy the client learns to live in reality
(*arugamama ni*—a Morita term) or to live properly and gently (*sunao
ni*—a Naikan term). The two terms share a sense of stable living
according to the matching of general life-principles and specific
situational realities or circumstances.

In terms of practice, the therapists in both styles of treatment exert
relentless pressure on the patient to behave as the therapy prescribes.
In Morita therapy the pressure may be more cold and overt. When the
patient exhibits the proper responses he feels a lessening of the pressure and, usually, a decline in his symptoms, as well. Repeated practice to improve one's form in tennis—to eliminate a bad habit during
the backhand stroke, for example—may be awkward, even painful, at
first, but after a time the result usually is a smoother, more comfortable
movement that complements the rest of one's game. In similar fashion
as the tennis coach, these therapists aim to correct an awkward life-
style. And clinical evidence suggests that, in terms of what they set out
to do, they are impressively successful.

Like Morita therapy, Naikan shades into religious experience. There
are therapeutic way stations along the Naikan path for those who
desire temporary relief from pressing personal difficulties and, further
along, resorts for deeper character change, but the ultimate destination
is satori or enlightenment for those who choose to travel that far. The
enlightenment of Naikan is the same as that of Zen and Morita therapy, yet different. The goal is selflessness. Zen brings about that
selflessness through "cool" meditation, discipline, and a critical prob-
ing of the rational flow of thoughts. Naikan utilizes a "warmer"
meditation focusing on the content (one's past recollections) rather
than the process (one's recollecting) and then working out the insights
in service to others.

In both cases one loses one's self. In both cases part of the journey
must be made alone, with occasional guidance from an experienced

traveler. In both cases the outcome is expressed in service. For the Naikan devotee the service itself is sufficient. It is an expression of faith and gratitude. For the Zen devotee and the Morita client, the service is another aspect of this moment's living, not to be particularly prized or desired; yet it turns out to be a major part of the client's existence. Existence creates the "importance" of service, not the mental processes of thinking about it or valuing it. I should warn the reader again that my thoughts here are the limited reflections of my level of understanding and experience with these two modes of seeking.

7_____Japanese Character
Another Look

I can associate humbly with others, finding myself to be powerless and helpless.
A Tottori Prison inmate

Throughout the chapters thus far I have inserted a minimum of interpretation. The book reports what Naikan therapists and clients do and what they say about their doing. The descriptions are backed by hours of observation and personal practice, by literature references, by quotes and questionnaires, photographs, and statistics. The goal was to make the main body of the text data-rich. What follows is different and either more or less important, depending on one's point of view. This chapter offers an organization of some of my thoughts on Japanese character after completing a period of intensive research on Naikan. I cannot spell out all the diverse sources of data that led to this formulation. The usefulness, if such there be, lies in the pulling together of ideas that seem to make sense of some aspects of Japanese character.

To write about national character at all is a perilous undertaking. The rich variety of life-styles among the population and the situated nature of human behavior make most nontrivial generalizations only partially true.

Another caveat is in order. As I grow older, the oppositional clichés of my culture become more and more meaningless to me. I look within myself and see a man both morally good *and* morally depraved. And so the artistic presentations of good whores and bad cops seem to me as futile as those of upstanding ministers and loathsome criminals. I peer within to find both introverted and extraverted impulses and orientations. I am not this *or* that. I am much of both or neither. I look around and see that there are clever but insensitive people who seem to exist hardly at all in the moral dimension, others who seem to be little aware of what goes on within or outside of themselves, and a few people who seem to be *beyond* being black or white, mentally sick or healthy, committed or indifferent. And individuals keep shifting back and forth among these categories.

I used to be surprised at the skill of many Japanese who were capable of pulling a bit of truth out of a grossly erroneous statement so that they could agree, in part, with the speaker. I marveled at the vagueness of their communications, analyzing them in terms of social expediency and immaturity and imprecision of thought. But now I am not nearly so sure of my analysis. At least for *human* topics and feeling statements, I suspect that vagueness best reflects what is knowable and communicable, that truths are blended and not subject to meaningful dissection and isolation, and that what is true of me sometimes is also false and that what is relevant is also irrelevant.

In *Morita Psychotherapy* (Reynolds, 1976) I examined Japanese national character in light of the insights provided by Morita's thought. The beam of the masculine, Zen-like Morita spotlight is sharply focused and rather cool. Naikan shows up Japanese character in an emotional light. And its play produces multiple shadows.

A few hours of observation were sufficient to open my eyes to the fact that Japanese psychotherapy in practice is much more flexible and humanistic than the rather rigid, harsh discipline one reads about in articles on the subject. Japanese writers describe what they consider to be an ideal treatment scheme. In many ways such a scheme is divorced from everyday therapeutic reality. (And, in my opinion, the everyday therapeutic reality is far superior to the "ideal" approaches one finds in the literature.) The Westerner who reads about Japanese social structure and culture may be misled in an analogous way. One reads that Japanese have trouble distinguishing between self and group, that there is no strong individual identity, that social relations and gift-giving are carefully balanced, that the people show great self-control and self-discipline. There is a note of truth in each of these described qualities but the reality is rather different from the image conjured up in the reading.

The description of the Japanese people in this chapter is neither flattering nor excessively harsh. It is unlike other descriptions and so must be scrutinized carefully for observer bias. Although at first the Japanese may be altogether unrecognizable in this sketch of their character, that may be because until now scholars have seen only what they expected to see and what they were expected to see.

The viewpoint expressed here follows from some basic questions surrounding Naikan therapy. Why should the already socially sensitive Japanese need a therapy that forces them to practice taking the points of view of significant others? Why should a people who supposedly keep social relationships carefully balanced need a therapy that requires them to examine and bring into balance their social relationships? And why should the Naikan point of view, so closely fitted to purported Japanese values, fade when the client returns to his everyday life away from a Naikan training center? At least two answers to the questions raised here are possible. The first is simply that Naikan is necessary for those social misfits who need special instruction or training in those Japanese social values and behavior that the normal Japanese employs automatically and well. The investigator who puts forth this answer looks at the criminals and delinquents and neurotics who do Naikan, and feels satisfied that these clients are just the ones who need resocialization into common Japanese norms and values.

The difficulty with such an answer is that it ignores the *majority* of Naikan clients who are normal Japanese and who do Naikan for self-insight and self-growth. Their mensetsu interview material is filled with the same kinds of confessions about much taken from others, little returned, much trouble caused to others through lies, stealing, inability to take the other's point of view, selfishness and self-centeredness, lack of self control, lack of gratitude, doubts about having been loved, and so forth. These Naikansha are normal or even superior members of Japanese culture in some respects. Where was the everyday taken-for-granted identity, the social balance, the self-sacrifice, the absence of an individual self-concept for these people? And why the talk of difficulty in *maintaining* a Naikan perspective and life-style in the midst of everyday life?

Put another way, just because Naikan is such a powerful force for attitude change, the task of maintaining the new perspective in the everyday world of Japan is extremely problematic. The difficulty for the Naikansha who completes a week of intensive meditation is very like that faced by people returning from a religious camp or retreat—the "coming-down-from-the-mountain" syndrome.

One might reasonably wonder why such a problem exists at all in this case. Certainly many scholars would argue that Naikan supports existing moral values and norms in Japan. Mothers are idolized; what is received and returned is calculated and balanced; self-sacrifice for others is valued; gratitude is encouraged; one's own faults are emphasized. Such ideals appear prominently in both Japanese culture and Naikan, it would seem. Then why should there be any difficulty maintaining a Naikan perspective within a society that apparently supports it so well?

A second, more radical resolution of the issues raised by these questions is that, contrary to some descriptions of Japanese national character, the Japanese are *not* basically group-oriented, other-centered, self-sacrificing; that Japanese society does not support such values; and that a therapy which does support them must swim upstream against a current of contrary habits and goals. The truth, perhaps, lies somewhere between these two answers to the questions posed by Naikan's existence. For more traditional views of Japanese character with valid but different emphases the reader is referred to Doi (1971), Nakane (1972), Iga (1968), Caudill (1959), and DeVos (1973) and Befu (1977). In the following pages the more radical view will be argued.

The reality of the situation as exposed by Naikan confessions and Naikan practice strikes hard at traditional descriptions of Japanese character and culture. Everyday life in Japan does *not* support Naikan perspectives and values. One is forced to look more deeply at the actuality of Japanese character. One must look at the differences between what people *say* they do and what they do *in fact*. Let us examine the other side of motherhood, giving, dependency, service, self-sacrifice, male dominance, and the group in Japan. A new picture of the Japanese will emerge—one that will lead, I hope, to a more balanced, realistic view than has been emphasized thus far.

The two themes that wind through this chapter are self-protection and control of others. With these themes I intend to thread together a number of observations and speculations. Both themes spring from a feminine perspective. In fact, if they are to be taken seriously, one must conclude that ideologically Japan is a female-dominated society. This domination, however, is covert. Let us consider how it appears to operate and how it is perpetuated.

Self-protection and covert control of others have been traits necessary for the survival of women and their offspring in most societies throughout the ages. From prehistoric times, males had to risk in order to succeed—in the hunt, in warfare, in movement from place to place. The female of this species, however, looked to the safety and protection of the family unit. First she had to protect her children, then herself, their immediate guardian, then her mate, who needed to be enticed to return consistently with the spoils of his foraging. The female had to devise means of turning the male's curiosity, energy, lust, and courage into family-centered channels. She was the great socializer in both a historical and a childrearing sense.

What resources did woman have at her disposal to draw man into long-term social relations? Certainly not physical strength; the female of the human species generally is smaller in stature and has less physical power than the male. Her sexual attractiveness, certain skills for making life more pleasant and comfortable, the ability to produce and rear children, these assets were hers. But also, perhaps, some characteristic psychological traits and skills, including the ability to show motherly warmth and affection, on occasion, to the adult male as well as to her children. And, I would argue, she also displayed the skills of manipulation of others that must be learned by any weaker member of a social relationship in which physical size, strength (and social values) limit the direct enforcement of desires and claims.

To be sure, there have been societies and families in which women were dominant, and the psychological characteristics outlined above were elaborated in many ways. Yet on the whole the skills of manipulation of others are learned in childhood from the mother, are honed in adolescence during mate-seeking, and are refined further during the rearing of one's own offspring. The smaller member's need for self-protection begins as early as the discovery that one can be hurt, and it grows as the days pass and one learns the variety of ways in which one can be hurt.

As for Japan, long years of relative isolation allowed the feminine values of self-protection and covert manipulation of others to permeate the social code. A frantic effort to reassert male dominance and values failed when Zen, samurai, and soldier gave way finally to the "economic animal" and the peace movement of modern Japan. On the other side of the Pacific, the frontier of America delayed the permeation of these feminine values for a while. On the frontier, risk and exploration often paid off from nature's abundance. But the frontiers seem to be of decreased interest these days—the sea, outer space, the mind—as the steady pressure builds to defend and protect limited resources and engage in the social-personal politics of the safe everyday life at home and at work. To break free from such pressure may be impossible and, perhaps, unwise. To succumb to it completely is to create a world of careful charade, the world of Japan in the 1970s.

FEAR OF FAILURE

Let us begin a detailed look at Japanese character with the problem of failure. For failure, or the fear of it, underlies much of the behavior of this people. In the English-conversation classroom, Japanese students hesitate to speak for fear of making a public mistake in this foreign language. Fear of making a social error prevents the Japanese from assertively approaching a foreigner to offer help when the foreigner appears to be, but may in fact not be, in some confusion at a train depot. Fear of the possibility of failure in any activity may make a Japanese doubly hesitant to take up an unfamiliar sport or hobby or ask someone for a date. As can be seen from these examples fear of failure can be translated into a kind of social rejection—one's mistake is exposed to public view and other's turn away because of it. An example of a paradigm for this fear in some cultures may be the woman's dread of losing her mate.

What is it about Japanese culture that makes failure or "misbehavior" so costly? There are two features which appear to be major contributors. One feature has to do with the way punishment is actually set up. The second has to do with the way it is perceived.

First, rewards come to the person who is sensitive to the needs of others in the groups to which the individual belongs. One who alienates his support groups is in great trouble in Japan. Not only socially but economically, politically (i.e., in the power he or she can wield), psychologically, and in practically every other sphere one can imagine, the isolated person is at great disadvantage in Japan. This reality problem is intensified by a psychological condition. Not only does the typical Japanese fear rejection for good practical reasons. He or she fears it far beyond even that. For most Japanese have had little experience with face-to-face confrontation, rejection, aggression, and the like. Particularly those within the family have been careful to shield each other from this unpleasantness.

Anzen na michi—The Safe Course

Self-protection is intimately intertwined with manipulation of others. Through control of others, one's own needs are met including the need for protection of one's self, one's possessions, and one's goals. A concrete example involves the mutual manipulation of the "kyoiku mama" (an education-oriented mother) and her student son. The kyoiku mama pushes her child to excel in his studies, knowing this path is a reasonable one to social and economic success in Japan. By working on his conscience, giving rewards, nagging, threats, by all means possible she directs her son toward the study goals she has set for him. On the other hand, the son, too, manipulates his mother. He may make demands for late snacks as he studies, an air conditioner for his room, books, vacations, or monetary rewards. He can require and get silence in the house, or stereo music, or a new color scheme in his study area. The result for the student is that failure to pass an entrance exam may mean more than merely inability to attend a particular university in a given year; it may mean loss of the student's basis for controlling his mother. That is, only with the hope of his success in studying could he influence her behavior. Should his failure provoke her to give up on his chances of entering the university, his leverage in their relationship changes considerably. A society that chooses a safety-first path, a low-risk course, is one in which there is a high social cost for failure.

The principle of Japanese in-family and in-group concern as opposed to public unconcern (Doi 1973) can be reduced to the simpler matter of resource control. Strangers are not likely to harm one or withhold resources to the degree family members can. On the other hand, outsiders must be watched carefully if they begin to impinge on one's life-space until one knows the proper ways of influencing them.

One might even consider the basis of shame, shyness, and stage fright to lie in the perceived (collective) power of strangers. Within some modern Japanese families, as fathers age and lose their power, wives and children may belittle the fathers and disregard their opinions to the degree socially permissible by their class and culture area in Japan.

The powerful impact of Naikan is evidenced by the Naikansha's willingness to confess past misdeeds not to the therapist (for that role relationship allows confession in any number of therapy styles and settings) but to a group of *strangers*, that is, fellow Naikansha during the closing zadankai. Murase, in a paper presented at the Twentieth International Congress of Psychology in 1972, reported on client perceptions of the Naikan therapists at the Nara Center. Using a modified, translated version of Strupp's Questionnaire (patient form), Murase found that clients perceived the therapists to be respectful of them, using natural speech that was not cold or formal, trustworthy, interested in helping, and occasionally giving assurance and direct advice. Compared with Strupp's American sample, these Naikansha appeared to be more concerned with being respected by the therapists than with being warmly accepted by them.

Such aspirations are true of social relations in general. While Americans tend to want to be liked (as conjunctive equals) Japanese tend to strive for respect from social others in various relative positions in the social hierarchy. Aiming for respect is somewhat more controllable (and, thus, safer), particularly in Japanese society, because "respectability" is based on what one does in terms of reasonably clear operating social norms. Being worthy of respect means being one who behaves properly. Aiming at being liked, on the other hand, is a much riskier proposition. In America, as in Japan, people have various personal preferences that they cannot control by their own efforts. And affection has a way of coming and going unpredictably. From adolescence Americans learn to handle the blows of not being liked by important others. The "handling" may be in healthy or unhealthy ways, but experiences of risk, success, and failure in this arena are common.

In Japan, when one is pressured into seeking warmth and acceptance, as in courtship, there is a higher element of tension because of lack of experience and some level of recognition of the lack of control in this area. So, given the choice, in therapy, teacher-student relations, even in marital relations the Japanese tend to opt for respect over affection. This characteristic may be changing, but the change will be slow because of the social risks involved.

Looked at from the perspective of defensive protectiveness, several other features of Japanese character take on new aspects. In Japan it is impolite to push forward one's own desires. "Would you prefer chicken or lamb for dinner tonight?" one asks the guest. "Oh, either will be fine. Which do you prefer?" is the reply. Polite, yes, but also safe. Self-revelation is dangerous. It gives a potential enemy ammunition to use against one in the future.

The *tateshakai*, the clear hierarchical social system described by Nakane (1972), provides important information about what power each society member wields. Thus, in any situation, through choice of terms of address and verb endings as well as through exchange of business cards and introductions, one quickly assesses the resources, authority, and sanctioning ability of a new acquaintance.

Ekman (1975), while showing Japanese and American audiences a stressful film about Australian subincision, photographed the facial expressions of the viewers. The results were "strikingly similar" in both settings. But, when interviewed, the Japanese, unlike the Americans, tended to mask their feelings of disgust and anger with polite smiles. To be expressive of face is a sign of immaturity in Japan, a characteristic feared by many neurotic Japanese and some mildly psychotic ones. To be expressive of face is to be vulnerable. One reveals to others the workings of one's heart. To be expressive in this way is to walk a path other than the safe one.

SHADOWS OF JAPANESE CHARACTER

Why are social relations fraught with anxiety and tension for the Japanese? Why are the symptoms of most neurotic patients centered around tension and self-consciousness in the presence of social superiors or persons of the opposite sex?

The most fundamental cause, I have argued (1976), is the Japanese person's sensitivity to the power exerted in his social sphere. Many other Japanese characteristics stem from the basic attention to power: fear of failure, *honne* and *tatemae* (inner feelings and social front), defensiveness and self-protectiveness, the use of social roles to protect the inner self, situational morality, gift-giving, the use of intermediaries, the Japanese language itself (its vagueness, its capacity for negation at the end of a sentence, its sensitivity to social status, etc.), positive feelings toward authority figures—the list could be extended indefinitely. One could also argue that the dark side of *amae* (the desire to be loved passively), of which Doi has made so much in explaining Japanese character, is the fear of power. *Amae no kozo* (Doi, 1973) may be reread profitably with a substitution of this power concern for the dependency argument Doi offers. The common features involve a recognition of the power in a social relationship (i.e., the resources controlled by self and by the other person) and the strategies to obtain those desired resources and avoid punishment. The resultant national character is one of attention to social detail, carefulness, and (depending on the power relationship in a given situation) sophisticated social skills such as tact, generosity, diplomacy, evasion, and hospitality.

A wide variety of Japanese traits make sense when one considers them aspects of what I have called above "anzen na michi" (the safe course), the way to achieve one's goals with minimal risk of criticism and punishment from powerful others. The Japanese love of natural beauty, their nostalgia for childhood, their admiration for American ways, all reflect this self-protective thought pattern. Who would criticize my finding beauty in a small flower or a rusted iron gate? Who would attack me for smiling as a small boy goes by engrossed in his first-grader's thoughts? And the favorable attitudes toward authority figures of traditional Japanese (in contrast with Americans' inbred distrust of any human power or authority) are well documented.

These safe positions, however, are no longer safe. Under the onslaught of Western assertiveness they will gradually change. Power must be doubted. Beauty must be protected consciously, not merely admired. Childhood, as old age, may come to be seen as a burden, a stage to be dreaded and overcome.

A situational morality is also safe. The element of self-protection, of defensiveness, takes precedence over some absolute law system. One's behavior can be flexibly extended in any direction depending on the conditions, those looking on, and their power over one's life. The danger, of course, is an aimless, wandering moral existence.

The problems generated by a power orientation of this sort are both social and personal. The personal problems, the ones with which I am most familiar, come from the suppression and ignoring of one's feeling states in order to achieve one's social goals. In other words, what one needs to do socially in order to protect one's interests may not conform with one's own emotions and desires. A subtle resentment builds up as a residue of the suppression of one's secret wishes. Of course, suppressing recognition of feeling states and social debts is not exclusively a Japanese trait. Americans practice such self-deception, too. For this reason, among others, Naikan has been effective in Western settings (see Chapter 8).

I believe that many Japanese wives are angry at their husbands, many workers angry at their supervisors, many students angry at their professors. They are also grateful, pleased, suspicious, and passively accommodating in these power relationships. But the anger may not be displayed under ordinary conditions. And the easiest course in lying to others (i.e., hiding one's anger) is to lie to one's self (I am not angry at my professor). The Japanese well know that the best act is one in which the actor's true feelings (on some level) merge with the part he plays (see Kiefer 1970).

122

DeVos (1980), too, has argued that many Japanese are angry at their parents and that Naikan allows them to reconstruct their memories of the past so that they need not deal with the realistic or childlike, unrealistic anger they would otherwise feel. Thus, the sacred family can be preserved. For some clients the benefits of Naikan may lie in this direction. However, the imperfections of one's parents are not denied in Naikan in Japan. Naikan is done, strictly speaking, not toward one's parents, but towards oneself in relation to parents and others.

Suppose that you are a hungry child and an adult approaches you with food. "Here, eat. You never appreciate what I do for you. Why don't you do as I tell you? I make all these sacrifices for you. Now I want you to do thus and so." You eat, but in a while you are hungry again. Along comes another adult with food for you. "Here, eat. I am happy to give you whatever I have. You are my beloved child." Again you eat, but time passes and you become hungry again. A third adult brings you food. "Eat if you want to. I really don't care whether you eat or not. You are nothing to me." Once again you eat. Most of our clients in Japan and in the United States focus on the attitude with which parents and other adults sustained them. In this example, they notice the manipulativeness, the love, the indifference. The Naikan therapist would say, without denying the variety of attitudes presented above, there is another reality that must not be ignored. That is the reality that the adult did bring the hungry food, and the child ate.

DeVos (1980) sees Naikan as creating idealized mythical parents as substitutes for the objectively imperfect actual ones. Yoshimoto sees Naikan as a means of recalling aspects of concrete events from the actual past which we have forgotten for our own convenience. Perhaps both are right.

Honne and *tatemae* or *omote* and *ura* (Doi 1973a), literally "front" and "back," are a sort of safety valve for this system. These concepts are evidence of the Japanese people's recognition of the split between what is and what must be socially. In substance, tatemae is one's social image, one's presentation of self to society; honne is one's "true" feelings, hidden away, rarely revealed. Another safety valve in the system is the use of social role to divorce one's self from the distasteful social tasks that are necessary for daily survival (Reynolds, 1976).

POTENTIAL PSYCHOLOGICAL COST

The emphasis on power in social relations generates characteristic personal difficulties. Several of the potential psychological problems associated with this social-power orientation, as well as the therapies designed to undo the personal damage, are considered next.

First, caution and social necessity can cause a Japanese person to be unaware that he truly *desires* to do, and enjoys doing, what is required of him in a given social situation. The joy of living is screened off by the "oughts" of living. This conception is not so foreign to Westerners. A party can become a chore rather than a pleasure. A visit to an aged relative may be socially required but it may also be a fine opportunity to catch up on family history and gossip.

Second, carefulness can limit the scope of exploration and inventiveness, and thus restrict the potential excitement and growth available to an individual. Under normal circumstances in Japan, a wedding ceremony or funeral ceremony must each be conducted according to its prescribed format. To be too innovative on such occasions would call one's social image into question. Similarly, a traditional gift is safest, conservative dress is often called for, and speech forms must be self-monitored for propriety. It is not that the Japanese do not explore or invent. Rather, they tend to do so only in non-power, or no-failure-possible, or no-safe-course-available contexts.

Third, the perceived necessity of presenting a positive image to powerful others requires the hiding of one's own faults, negative feelings, disagreements, and misdeeds. As Mowrer (1964) has pointed out, concealing one's misdeeds from others takes great energy and attention and makes social relationships exhausting and distasteful. After all, the more one meets with others the more chance there is that they might discover one's secrets. Constant self-monitoring and censoring is a bothersome task even when routinized in daily habit patterns.

Fourth, there is the danger that the neurotic person in his narrow world will come to see his lifeway as the only one available to him—that he has no choices. "This is the way I am: neurotic, shy, a failure, unmarried," he may think. Particularly when others' lives appear to be synchronized so smoothly with the prescribed routines for their social lives, the person who feels he does not mesh smoothly may despair of ever fitting into an appropriate niche.

Fifth, avoidance of confrontation with powerful others produces a weak self-image and low resistance to forceful, assertive behavior. One avoids unpleasant problems, ignores them, flees from them rather than endure the momentary pain involved in solving them.

Naikan psychotherapy can be seen to concern itself primarily with the first and third of these problems, Morita therapy with the second and fourth and fifth. However, both Japanese therapies handle all of these problems in characteristic ways.

The issue of what one wants to do as opposed to what one has to do is the underpinning of Freudian thought. The personal libidinous desire, the id, confronts the social limits, the conscience, the superego. Morita therapy sidesteps this issue (as does Zen Buddhism) by advising that one accept feelings, any feelings, as they are while going about doing what needs to be done. What needs to be done is not merely what the superego dictates or what conformity to social mores demands (as many Westerners mistakenly believe Morita therapy to require), but what is called for by each moment's living. Morita's method is based on a trust of one's inner sense of the moment's demands, a kind of disciplined, deepened ego, in Freudian terms.

Naikan grapples directly with the issue of desire vs. social limits. Naikan argues that if you look deeply enough, *what you have to do* as a social being is also *what you truly desire to do*. There is no conflict. Society demands that you return to others as they have given to you. Naikan aims to show the client that when he did not live up to this social demand he felt diminished and was hurting himself as well as others. Certainly, on looking back on past self-centeredness the client perceives his own smallness, cowardice, ineffectiveness, inferiority.

When one's desire is to give one's self to others, he is playing a social game he can win. Trying to *manipulate* powerful others in one's life is a difficult and uncertain business. Ultimately, others are not controllable. They can choose to balk, rebel, lash out. On the other hand, giving one's self to others is relatively controllable and possible. That self-sacrifice is Naikan's goal.

The caution that limits a client's life until he narrows his focus down to his own internal state, his own room, his own bed, is tackled head-on by Morita therapy. Again, the strategy employed is to have the client accept his fears about venturing out while venturing out nonetheless. The confidence to do so will come *after* successful venturing, *not before*. The natural rewards of successful accomplishment will sustain the behavior; but, rewards or not, exploration must continue.

As noted above, the pitfall of self concealment is the fundamental problem attacked by Naikan. The client is required to examine himself harshly, like a prosecuting attorney. His errors must be admitted to himself, his therapist, and (often) his fellow Naikansha clients. Public confession frees the energy that was invested in concealing past errors. The burden of supporting a strong ideal image is removed.

The fourth problem is a sort of fatalistic giving up on the self. The image one presents to others is one of weakness and oversensitivity. There appear to be no choices in one's circumscribed environment. Morita therapy challenges such an attitude. Moment-by-moment choices are immediately available, the Moritist holds. In the past the decision to avoid exploring all options was made over and over until avoidance became automatic. The client must relearn the options in his everyday life and make responsible choices among them. Naikan undermines this superficial self-abandonment with a deeper, existential one. And choices reappear.

The fifth problem, what Westerners might call a lack of ego strength, is handled in Morita therapy (and in Naikan, as well) by firmly directing the patient to focus on his purpose. During Naikan this purpose is deeper and deeper self-reflection, despite the welling up of feelings.

Perhaps an added word about isolation is in order here. There is a sense in which the group-oriented Japanese are among the loneliest people I know. Surrounded by work-mates, family, friends, and neighbors, locked into social reciprocity on every side, the hurting Japanese individual often finds nowhere to turn for complaint and comfort. To pour out one's troubles is to burden the listener. The listener is reminded of life's tragedy. He may feel pressured to act in behalf of the suffering complainant. Certainly, the listener would be expected to empathize and sympathize with the sufferer. All this unpleasantness is likely to disturb the listener and to place a strain on the relationship between the two—or so the suffering Japanese is likely to feel. Thus, he suffers silently, alone, doing his best to conceal the whole tragic conflict from those around him. It is the rule to hear from neurotic patients that prior to treatment no one knew about their symptoms (which may have continued for many years).

The opportunity to unload during the mensetsu interviews often results in initial cathartic outpouring of past suffering quite outside the framework of what was received, returned, and what trouble was caused others. Such catharsis is permitted, even encouraged in some settings, within limits. Should it continue beyond the first few interviews, it is considered to interfere with genuine Naikan meditation. The client is gently reminded that it is not acceptable to do "Gaikan" (*external* observation).

For some, not all, Japanese, these personal problems are some of the costs involved in being culture members. They are potential dangers associated with a social system that requires much of the individual in order to keep the system running. American culture presents a different range of dilemmas for its members. Insensitivity, blatant self-centeredness, isolation, and the paradox of valued freedom of behavioral expression of feelings within the social bounds of decorum are typical shadows of American culture paralleling those described for Japan.

CHILDREARING

Perhaps the impact of Naikan therapy has something to do with the factor of unconditional love. The child in Japanese culture is loved unconditionally. Whatever the child does he/she is cherished, taught, guided, and listened to—the center of family members' attention. However, as the child grows older that love and attention is gradually changed to a pattern in which the love is offered only as the person conforms to certain expectations and meets certain obligations. This pattern—one in which generous offerings are made until a child/client/student/visitor/disciple is caught up by interest in a subject or the desire to join a group and the offerings are then replaced by strict pressures and demands—is common in Japan. It may be part of the reason why tourists and other guests are treated so well in Japan (they do not stay long enough to reach the second stage). This two-stage process provides an effective method of behavior shaping. Naikansha in Japan do turn up recollections of extreme parental self-sacrifice during their childhood.

In *Morita Psychotherapy* I outlined the position of the Japanese mother as the nurturing giver and controller of the child, the model of social sensitivity. The father played little part in that analysis, as he plays little part in the childrearing process. I find it rather annoying to hear of the deprived Japanese father who works and sacrifices only to be shut out of the mother-child coalition. We all contribute to our family structure and gain something from it. Just as there is collusion by some psychiatric patients to allow hospital staff control (and responsibility for) their lives, so in Japan many husbands and fathers are quite content to encourage the mother-child collaboration that isolates them. Problems with the child can be pinpointed as the mother's failure in responsibility. The male is free to seek role-specific satisfactions outside the family—at work and elsewhere.

Dr. Kondo Akihisa (a psychoanalyst and Morita therapist) treats both American and Japanese patients; some of the latter include dropouts from Naikan therapy. He finds more hostility toward the mother and finds it closer to the surface in Americans. It is not that anger and resentment toward the mother is absent in Japanese. Rather it seems to be more difficult to tap and express. Perhaps one reason for the difference lies in control tactics employed by mothers in these two cultures. Of course, within both cultures there are wide individual variations. Yet on the whole it appears that the American mother uses confrontation, direct opposition of will, and physical force more often than the Japanese mother to bring about behavioral compliance in the child. The Japanese mother utilizes bribes, misdirection of attention, explanation, and a purposely projected image of nurturance and knowledge of the child's needs and desires to assure compliance (Reynolds 1976).

Taking the argument back a step further Kondo argues that indirect control methods are employed by Japanese mothers because their overt access to recognized power within the family is severely limited. They operate from weakness yet are required to control their children.

The American mother, conversely, is in a relatively stronger position, aligned with her husband, supported in her child control. As a result, she is socially permitted to exert that control openly and directly.

Many of the Japanese youth coming for treatment today exhibit an attitude called "shirake," a sort of blanching or fading of their perspective on the world. Nothing excites their interest particularly; there is no drive to succeed. As long as one gets by, that is sufficient. Gone are the days of youth with prominent identity crises. Who am I? What do I expect from life? What does life expect from me? Such questions, however anguished, imply a sort of commitment to life and self, a need to examine one's purposes and goals, to find one's place in the world. For the youth of *shirake*, such questions are unimportant. Who cares?

Perhaps the roots of *shirake* lie in the worldwide trend of reducing the amount of consumption. Now is a time of cutting back, holding on. The young persons of today cannot win at the game of success played by their parents. No one wants to play a game they are sure to lose. So they spurn the game altogether. The big ego asks for everything. These Japanese youth ask for a minimally comfortable existence but offer nothing in return.

What Yoshimoto seems to have done, as Kondo Akishisa points out, was to take the ideal qualities of love and wisdom attributed to Amidha Buddha by Jodo Shinshu believers and to bring these qualities "down to earth" in the sense of personifying them in each Naikansha's mother. The elegance of this strategy is that the application of these characteristics is no longer on some abstract level; rather they become visible, concretized, modeled in the lives of people each Naikansha knows. To say "I am loved by Amidha" is one thing. To say "My mother loved me enough to pack special lunches with my favorite rice balls each time we went on a class outing in the third grade" is quite another. The former is a string of words explainable by another string of words, often divorced from everyday reality in the mind of the believer. The latter happened, is recalled, and has a feeling tone associated with its recollection.

The problem with the *"terra*fication" of these ideal qualities in the mother is that for some Naikansha, the behavior of their mothers (or mother surrogates) did not conform in reality to these ideal qualities of love and wisdom. There are "bad" mothers in Japan too.

The frequency with which such disturbed and disturbing mothers actually appear from culture to culture is unknown. However, it has been my experience in Japan and in America that mothers who appear deficient to Naikansha at the beginning of Naikan turn out to be seen with many more positive qualities by the time Naikan is completed. Moreover, I have rarely encountered a person who did not find some relatively positive parental figure while growing up, whatever the faults of his/her biological mother. As noted in the previous section, whatever the twisted motives and manipulations of parent figures, the reality also includes the feeding and clothing of the child, shelter and care during illness—some consistency sufficient to allow the child's survival to become a Naikansha. That degree of effort and commitment cannot often be denied.

One frequently sees parents explaining even to small children why they are to do or refrain from doing something. From an early age, the assumption is that if the child *truly understands* he will behave properly. This assumption extends throughout Buddhism in its various cultural elaborations and appears, of course, in Shinshu-based Naikan therapy. When the Naikansha truly understands himself, behavior problems of all sorts will be straightened out.

Perhaps that assumption about understanding is one of the reasons why impulse pressure (to buy, for example) is high in some Japanese. If one allows oneself to stop and consider the situation, one may not act in that immediately self-gratifying way. The inner voices of reason (parents, social mores) are strong. To pause is to invite conflict and resistance.

The theme of impulse controlled by reason runs through many Japanese films. In a typical story line the rash youth wants to rush out and sacrifice himself to kill the oppressive tyrant. He is warned by a wiser adult that to do so would be to play into the tyrant's hand. That impulse to hurt a powerful figure is strongly suppressed in Japan. And it is consequently an impulse that when actualized in behavior takes particularly volatile and extreme form. Such suppressed rage has its roots in the mother-child relationship, one might suspect, just as the self-sacrificing reciprocity of Naikan has its roots in the same dyad. The threat of losing the all-giving other, if the older child allows his rage to demonstrate itself, is one of the first steps on the "safe course" in life.

Blindness to one's concealed rage is, of course, not a quality exclusive to the Japanese. But there is a sort of selective inattention which is employed with a frequency peculiarly Japanese. The Japanese people seem to be able to ignore large chunks of contradicting reality while focusing in on some smaller segment. It simply is not true that the housewife I interviewed one morning in Nara returned nothing to her husband during the period covered in her Naikan reflection as she said. She undoubtedly cooked and presented him meals, laid out his clothes, prepared his bath, and so forth. Perhaps she rarely (or possibly never) felt these acts to be repayment from her gratitude. Now she cannot see the acts at all in her attention to what she received from him, his hard days at work, and the trouble she caused him with his mother.

In Ekman's (1975) study mentioned above the Japanese were relatively unskillful at identifying photographed facial expressions of anger and shame, and generally did poorly on negative emotions (distress, disgust, sadness, fear) as opposed to positive ones. It would appear that they just did not want to see those unpleasant things, and they did not. Perhaps an unwillingness to view the supportive family in a negative light is one of the reasons why Freudian psychoanalysis never received a serious trial from the Japanese people.

More Myths and Countermyths

Currently, there are many articles and books about Japanese character and culture. In particular, books written by foreigners emphasizing differences between the Japanese and other peoples are popular. On television a Canadian author gave his opinion that the Japanese are eager to read such descriptions of themselves because they are gradually losing their differentness, becoming more and more like Europeans or Americans. Such books preserve the illusion of a unique Japanese character.

Another explanation is possible. For a culture in which image presentation and self-protection are primary, one needs constant reassurance that one's presentation of self is successful. When one's life-course and moment-by-moment activities are determined by the presentations of views of those around one, there is a continuous need to monitor those views as well. It is a kind of "floating world" in modern Japan.

The myth of the passive, patient, obedient Japanese was exploded quickly at the Nara Center, as in any setting where actual observation would be possible. The variety of time-fillers employed, expecially in the first few days of Naikan meditation, provokes admiration at the ingenuity and imagination of human beings. As I made the rounds I noticed people sleeping, writing (usually in a small notebook to keep their recollections straight for mensetsu), staring out the window, reading books, brushing teeth, making frequent trips to the bathroom, laundering small items in the sink, playing with transient insects, smoking, and conversing. But the weight of those pastimes is too great for the temporal line to support. Most such behaviors disappear after a few days or, alternatively, the person decides to leave, finding the amount of time to be filled greater than his resources for filling it—*unless he actually does Naikan*. Herein lies some of the effectiveness of the method. The motivation to do Naikan lies at least in part in the lack of any other rewarded method of filling the great span of subjective time.

Kato and others have looked at the traditional living space in the Japanese house and questioned the existence of a concept of private space. This concept of private space may be recent in Japanese history but it certainly appears to have taken hold. The space behind the byobu screen (and even the way the byobu was arranged—the angle, the placement of both halves) was ordered to fit the desires of the Naikansha much in the same way a hospitalized Western patient orders his bed, nightstand, and tray table.

Finally, the myth of the laconic, silent Oriental is simply divorced from reality. The Japanese are *obsessed* with words, one might argue. Scholarly meetings devote much time to word derivations and relabeling in contrast to presentation of new findings. Words are "safe," in that the scholar engages in a game of definitions, a game harder to challenge than one in which data are presented and opinion emerges during interpretation.

Similarly, psychotherapies (including Naikan) offer the patients memories, slogans, catch-phrases for ordering their experiences. That Naikan is a talking therapy cannot be denied. From mensetsu to zadankai speech is prominent in the treatment.

Other aspects of Japanese culture: the historical creation of regional dialects for secrecy, the presence of a religion (Zen) aimed at crushing the everyday world of words while subtly substituting a Buddhist vocabulary, the high literacy rate, much word-play in conversation—one could go on and on—point to the importance of words in everyday life in this East Asian country.

It would be unfair, though, to omit a balancing statement about the complementary Japanese *distrust* of speech and its intellectual well-springs without some validating action and "body knowledge" experience. The Japanese, too, have the notion that "talk is cheap."

SELF-DECEPTION AND NAIKAN

The social sensitivity of the Japanese must result in a sort of self-deception for ego survival. When nearly every act is defined in terms of its social consequences, each spoken sentence formed in terms of the listener's social relationship and the sentence's social effect, a Japanese could be immobilized by the sheer burden of social calculation necessary prior to emitting a behavior. And, of course, *not* acting has social consequences, too. A sort of selective attention, then, becomes necessary to carry out the business of everyday life. The Japanese social being focuses on some basic social grammatical forms: expressing relationships through pronoun and verb forms, resorting to vagueness when a direct statement may endanger a relationship, keying in on stereotypical situations such as who goes first, host-guest behavior, nonthreatening behavior, nonprying behavior, and so forth.

An interesting feature of this other-directed behavior is that consequences occur both for the other and for the actor himself. Why did I give her flowers? For her surprise and joy, to mark a level in our relationship, to encourage her to think well of me, to demonstrate that

131

I am the sort of person who gives flowers, and so on. The motivations and effects of any social act are so numerous as to be incalculable in the pace of daily social life. But it is precisely such complex analyses of motivations and social consequences that fill the pages of Japanese novels from modern times (Mishima, Tanizaki, Kawabata) back at least to Natsume Soseki and probably much earlier.

Social values ascribe merit to the person who acts unselfishly for the good of his family, his company, his friend, and the like. Yet behaviors are complexly motivated and the Japanese are well aware of this complexity. The solution adopted by most Japanese most of the time has been to ignore the selfishly motivated elements of daily action. Why did you give her the flowers? She is a nice person. My sister asked me to give them to her. She likes flowers. She seemed sad recently; I wanted to cheer her up. These are the sorts of verbalized motivations elicited when one asks such a question. And, I believe, there is no conscious attempt to deceptively slant the response. Rather, the other category of self-serving responses is suppressed, ignored—kept out of awareness—for the sake of expedient social action and for the sake of ego preservation.

By ego preservation I mean nothing more than sustaining a positive self-concept. The person who acts for the benefit of others is well-thought-of in Japan, by others and by himself. Just as one wants to see others in a good light, one wants to see oneself favorably, too.

Before going further I shall contrast this style of being with that of Americans. Americans, I believe, simply are less aware of the social consequences of everyday acts. Moreover, they are much more willing to ascribe to others and to themselves selfish motivations. The old-hand American in Japan may see Japanese gift-giving as a setup for later favors and return gifts. The newcomer simply takes them gratefully with no awareness of the social obligations that go with them. I am reminded of the study carried out years ago in which Japanese ascribed their failure in some area to inability rather than unwillingness. Americans, on the other hand, preferred the excuse that they *could* do some task but did not want to (a very nonsocial response) (DeVos 1973).

To Japanese eyes, then, the American seems remarkably free, behaving with apparent openness in all sorts of social situations. In fact, the American may be simply processing less social data and may be more willing to talk about selfish motivation when that seems appropriate. The vaunted kindness of Americans to Japanese visitors in the U.S. is probably a combination of host-guest courtesy and the Japanese assumption that the guests' needs have been thoughtfully considered and, where ignored, were believed by the hosts to be

132

unimportant. In fact, the guests' needs in such areas may not have been considered by the hosts at all.

For the Japanese, I have sketched the outlines of a people who are socially sensitive yet must ignore and suppress recognition of self-profiting motivations and acts in order to be well-thought-of by others and by themselves. Or so they think.

Naikan therapy changes all that. It forces the Naikansha to look clearly at the social side that he has hidden from himself. While in relative isolation, he must reflect on how much he received or took from others, how little he returned to them, and how much trouble he caused him. This perspective is contrary to the view of social life ordinarily employed by the Japanese. It is not uncommon to hear initial denials and failures to recall any trouble caused others.

At first I could not understand the full purpose of reflecting on lies and stealing or on calculating the amount of money one wasted during years of alcoholism. These topics were not "balanced" in the traditional Naikan format of things received and things returned. These topics failed to show the love received while one was hurting others and using their resources.

Only gradually did I come to realize that the power of Naikan lies not so much in love remembered but in love expressed in the therapy-present, and in the cathartic freedom produced through this social communication about a suppressed side of the self. The tears are not only tears of remorse but more often tears of relief at being able to think and speak about the self-centered, voracious aspect of one's identity. (Again, DeVos in a personal communication notes the parallel with the conversion experience in Western Christianity.) And the response to such verbalization is never the dreaded rejection and expressions of disgust and social superiority. Rather the result is continued acceptance, gratitude, appreciation. During mensetsu the therapist bows humbly, listens gratefully. Yoshimoto specifically warns against a haughty demeanor in therapy. The post-Naikan meetings provide further opportunity for acceptance to be demonstrated following confession. What a revelation this result must be to the Naikansha! Throughout their lives this part of their character was kept hidden even from themselves. Now it stands revealed.

It is typical of Japanese therapies and culture that such self-revelation occurs in a social setting (Zen satori must be confirmed by a *roshi* master) and is turned to social ends. The self-revelation is not merely to free the person through discovery of a new side of the self. Rather he is to go forth to begin repaying his social debt all the while remembering this darker side of his character. Just as the Zen monk who achieves satori chooses to remain on earth to help others achieve it, so personal growth is turned to social ends in Japanese culture. But, then, to do less would be less than humanity at its finest, some would say. I am at my best when giving myself completely to others, they hold. Such a creed would be understood by Western Christians as readily as Eastern Buddhists.

ON SHAME AND THE SEARCH FOR THE JAPANESE

Benedict in *The Chrysanthemum and the Sword* (1946), held that cultures could be classified into those that are shame-oriented and those that are guilt-oriented. The shame-oriented culture, of which Japan was considered a classic type, was presumed to lack norm internalization, to lack guilt, and to lack absolute standards of behavior. Control and conformity were presumed to be ensured through external social pressure. Elsewhere the Japanese have been described as "weak in 'sin-consciousness' " and "sensitive in 'shame-consciousness' " (Nakamura 1964), and having "little consciousness of guilt, lack of profound hatred of sin" (Yamamoto 1964). Others, however, took issue with any interpretation of Japanese character as lacking in guilt. DeVos (1973) appropriately pointed out the capacity of Japanese mothers to manipulate their children by means of guilt. Doi (1973b) linked extreme guilt in the Japanese to betrayal of one's social group.

In fact the audio tapes of Naikan mensetsu are filled with expressions of guilt. And the guilt expressed is not unlike that of contemporary Westerners. Although the social and personal *consequences* of misdeeds are stressed in Naikan (as in Western liberal Christian settings), there are exchanges in which the participants talk as if gambling, smoking, lying, and the like are "bad" in the sense of some *absolute standards*. Thus, even the subtler distinction between "Western guilt" (standard-based) and "Japanese guilt" (situation-based) seems to break down in this Naikan setting. Leaving aside the case of the subgroup of Japanese Christians, even within this Buddhist setting guilt as well as shame are clear elements of the Japanese participants' character structure.

The problem here, as I see it, is not in the lack of "fit" of Benedict's formulation with the reality of the Japanese cultural setting but with the dichotomized analytical concepts of American science. Japan is not shame-oriented or guilt-oriented; it is both.

INTROVERSION-EXTRAVERSION RECONSIDERED

Much social-science research is based on the premise that extraversion (outer-directedness or other-directedness or group-orientation) is a polar opposite of introversion (or inner-directedness or individualistic orientation) and that a person's characterological makeup can be plotted along a continuum with these two poles as reference points. If a person is highly *self*-oriented he cannot be highly *group*-oriented, according to this line of thinking. The Japanese, for example, are said to be highly group-oriented. "An individual in Japan, in a profound sense, exists only in terms of the groups to which he belongs, and there is little separate identity apart from such contexts" (Caudill 1959). Similar quotes can readily be found throughout the literature on the Japanese. Yet I find Japanese to be, in some respects, at least as self-centered as Westerners. Other scholars, too, have recognized the self-focus while emphasizing the other-focus aspect.

My observations of the Japanese lead me to believe that there are culture members who are both extremely group-oriented and extremely self-oriented, sensitive to both socially instigated and self-generated cues. If they were otherwise there would be no need for the therapies like Naikan, Morita's methods, or Zen, all of which aim at helping extremely self- and other-centered neurotics lose the self. Probably the most common neurotic syndrome in Japan is social uptightness—what is he/she thinking of *me*?

One can find in the literature formulations of Japanese character which suggest that individuals find it hard to distinguish self from surrounding group members, that the self is merged with a group identity. In fact group identification is, in most instances, strongly counterbalanced by purely personal desires and goals. Being a group member is a safe, self-protective course in Japan that generally helps one achieve one's private ends. When Naikan advises the client to *truly* merge with the surrounding others, there is great difficulty and no little resistance toward movement in that ego-dissolving direction.

It is said that "ma," the space in an Oriental ink painting contains much meaning and esthetic value. Such can be said equally of the spaces in Japanese social contacts. In conversation, when the listener's head-nodding and its verbal equivalents stop, the speaker knows something is wrong. In letter writing, when the letters suddenly cease in mid-exchange, something is wrong. When friends or neighbors stop visiting, when gifts and phone calls stop coming, an important communication has been made.

The immediate interpretation in Japan is that there is something *I* have done to provoke others to break off the flow of signals that have indicated all was well between us. This attitude is both extremely humble (and group-oriented) and extremely egocentric (self-oriented). It is humble in that the assumption is that I am at fault, that my unintended error has caused the group's problem. It is egocentric in that the supposition exaggerates my control over the relationship, my power to disrupt it, the influence of my behavior in others' decisions.

The Japanese use role behavior, I believe, to insulate or protect personal identity, not to suppress it. That is, when operating appropriately in their social roles, they fulfill their obligations to the significant social others in the setting without committing themselves to an expression of their personal thoughts and feelings. Thus, a principal who commits suicide following the accidental death of a schoolchild on the school's playground is *preserving* his personal reputation, his self-image, while punishing the social-role occupant who failed as principal.

This notion of social role as a protective shell around personal identity allows us to view the Japanese as both totally committed, self-sacrificing group members (as occupiers of roles) and narcissistically self-centered individuals (as users of roles to distance the self from socially required behaviors and values.) In fact, this dimension of high self-orientation *and* high other-orientation, as opposed to low social focus and low self-focus, makes sound theoretical sense in terms of our understanding of the social construction of self-image. An extension of the symbolic interactionists' position (that of G. H. Mead, Cooley, and others) might be that those infants (and children and adults) who sensitively respond to signals from significant others develop a stronger, clearer perception of self than those who are less sensitive. Thus, we arrive at the Japanese who responds with hyperawareness to external *and* internal signals, that is, we arrive at one who is both introverted and extraverted.

In sum, once more, the Naikan setting provided a situation in which some traditional interpretations of Japanese character would benefit from some change in emphasis. The Naikansha clients seemed to display both shame *and* guilt; they appeared to be both self-oriented *and* other-oriented. I have argued that in these latter cases the discrepancies lie in our dichotomized categories requiring an "either-or" conceptualization when a "both-and" description seems more consistent with observations.

Throughout this chapter my argument about Japanese character and culture has emphasized divergence from traditional views. A wider perspective might incorporate the traditional views presented in the literature and the divergent position taken in this work. One learns over time a healthy distrust for the ability of one's own words to depict a reality that changes moment by moment, vantage point by vantage point.

8_____ Naikan for Westerners

AMERICAN CHARACTER

The few Americans who tried Naikan in Japan and taped their mensetsu interviews shared some characteristic difficulties. Noteworthy was their tendency to see social relations as ones among equals with shared responsibilities and shared faults. They were quite willing to see their lacks in giving and their troublemaking for others, but they perceived collusion in the processes. At the very least the others chose to stay in the relationships, the Americans argued, so they must have been getting something out of them. Self-centeredness was assumed for all parties by the American Naikansha; the model seems to be that the alter's self-centeredness leads him/her to make demands of the client just as the client makes demands of alter. The responsibility for achieving a dynamic balance in the relationship lies with both members, each asserting his own claims. It is as if there were figuratively a fixed-center fulcrum and each actor adds weights to his own side until a satisfactory balance is achieved.

The Japanese Naikansha, however, saw the responsibility as that of the Naikansha alone. When he received from others it was his moral duty to repay at least as much as he received. Again, using a scale analogy, it is as if each actor had a fixed (not necessarily equal) set of weights. The first actor moves the fulcrum to increase the leverage of the other. Now it is the other's responsibility to move the fulcrum back, favoring the first actor, and so forth.

Americans showed more mistrust of authority figures than the Japanese meditators. They more often questioned the motives of others in giving them something. The Japanese tended to suppress recognition of and talk about improper motives in others.

American independence showed clearly during Naikan interviews. Individual effort was emphasized, while crediting others for one's success seemed more difficult for Americans.

Viewing one's life in a black or white, right or wrong, moral system seemed to cause these Westerners trouble. They kept looking for intermediate grays, and felt uncomfortable with the pressure to state clearly and without qualification that they had exploited specific others in specific ways. Partly this discomfort may have something to do with the contrasting black or white attitude these Americans seemed to take toward factual reality. They wanted to make formulations about themselves that would be "true" from an objective viewpoint. The Japanese Naikansha seem to view truth in a more relative way, as "fitting" in a particular situation at a particular time. Philosophically, of course, the case concerning the subjective nature of truth can be argued both ways. The different approaches to truth were apparent as I contrasted my efforts, typical of the aggressive Western scholar who aims at finding errors and gaps in the theories and studies presented to me by Naikan therapists, with the efforts of the Japanese, who seemed to be looking for ways to make sense of, find worth in, and discover areas of common ground in my speech. Though I automatically assumed that they sometimes made errors, their attitude seemed to be that the locus of miscommunication was not in my errors but in their difficulty in understanding what it was that I was saying.

NAIKAN IN THE WEST

Elsewhere I have written of the cross-cultural adaptability of a Japanese psychotherapy (Reynolds and Kiefer 1977), of the steps necessary for adoption of an Eastern therapy in the Western world (Reynolds 1978), and of the divergent assumptions underlying Eastern and Western therapies which make for difficulties in communication about them across cultures (Reynolds 1980).

Although Naikan appears to be based on panhuman principles of reciprocity (see Chapter 6), there remain certain practical problems in applying the method within Western cultural contexts. Finkbeiner (personal communication) reported that current interests in various meditation forms made easier his trials of Naikan within the West German penal system. Similarly, those of my clients at the ToDo Institute who are fascinated by things Japanese and intrigued by Buddhist ideas are more likely to agree to undergo a trial period of Naikan.

Resistance comes from many professional colleagues. The resistance, at least overtly, is based on theoretical rather than experiential or experimental grounds. Japanese culture is so different from ours, they hold. Childrearing practices are different; dependency continues as an acceptable pattern into adulthood. Between our cultures concepts of obligation, social sensitivity, and humility differ greatly in degree, if not in kind, they argue. How can a therapy springing out of such a unique cultural context have relevance for Western clients?

Those few Westerners who have undertaken intensive Naikan report it to be a profoundly moving and valuable experience—a benchmark in their lives. Of course, they represent a self-selected sample of presumably atypical representatives.

The question of the usefulness of Naikan in the West is, as I have written above, the basis of a testable hypothesis. So far, the numbers are too few and the sampling inadequate to permit a serious evaluation.

My own introduction to a week of intensive Naikan was described in *The Quiet Therapies* (Reynolds 1980). It is repeated here because it is the most detailed published account of a Westerner's Naikan experience.*

After brief introductions, I was asked to listen to a set of taped instructions that included excerpts from a second-grader's Naikan training. The tape is commonly played for beginning clients. It is simple and effective in that the child's questions, difficulties, and responses are ingenuous and to the point.

Besides the instructions regarding the periodic interview format, Naikan technique, house rules, and so forth, two additional points stand out in my mind. One was that the boy on the tape was unable to recall *meiwaku* (difficulties he had caused others). He was repeatedly encouraged to examine his past more deeply. Thus, I learned early that failure to recall inconveniences I had caused others would not be tolerated in this setting. The second point, that initial boredom and difficulty with Naikan meditation would be replaced around the third day with increased skill and deeper Naikan, has important theoretical implications. In fact, this phenomenon does occur for many clients. This preparatory piece of information not only effectively "inoculates" clients against the discouragement engendered by initial problems in practicing Naikan, but it also builds the image of the sensei as an experienced and knowledgeable guide in this area. One result is, I believe, increased client suggestibility.

I was taken upstairs at 3:45 P.M. to a large tatami mat room; assigned a corner; and provided with a tufted cushion, a flat pillow, a byobu (folding screen), and a hanger for my clothes. I was shown where the sleeping mattresses and cleaning gear were stored and where the toilet and washbasin were to be found.

I began at 4:05. My thinking was at first vague and diffused, but gradually I began to focus on the period and person assigned to me by Yoshimoto Sensei. At 4:50 the sensei came for my first mensetsu (Naikan interview). In the ritualized format of greeting and confession I told him of what I had received, what I had returned, and the troubles I had caused my mother during the period before grammer school. I

*The account that follows is taken from David K. Reynolds, *The Quiet Therapies* (Honolulu: University Press of Hawaii, 1980), pp. 56–64, and is used with permission.

mentioned, for example, my dislike of margarine. My preference prompted my mother to serve expensive butter at my meals—a kindness I had not properly appreciated before. I specifically did not mention my recollection that she tried (unsuccessfully) several times to pass off margarine in butter wrappings as the genuine article. I had begun to slant my description, if not my recollection, of the past. At 5:20 the sensei brought each client his meal on a tray. My sweet potatoes were covered with butter.

Naikan continued. I could hear children playing outside. A radio or tape recorder was playing downstairs. Two clients spoke quietly to one another in disregard of the rule of silence. I was having difficulty remembering the point to be presented in Japanese at the mensetsu as I moved from memory to memory in English. At 9:05 P.M. we four clients emerged from behind our screens. We laid out the bedding in silence. In a few minutes I slept.

Before 5:00 A.M. on Monday, the speaker system high on the wall of our room erupted with the sounds from a Naikan tape. These tapes contained information about Naikan successes, excerpts from particularly moving interviews with clients and their families, songs about mothers, and so forth. We swept the room and wiped the floor with a damp cloth in silence. Someone cleaned the toilet. We washed our faces and returned to meditation. At 5:40 the sensei came for his fourth interview. By that time I had learned a great deal about the way I anchor the past in my memory. I found that I coded the past, not so much in terms of the years in which events occurred, but in terms of houses I had lived in, cars I had ridden in as a child, jobs I had held, schools I had attended, and people I had known. The years of junior high school ran together, but they were distinct from the years of high school and college.

Another tape began at 6:00 A.M. and continued through breakfast until 6:25 A.M. I could hear the sounds of a nearby client flipping the pages of a book and taking notes. The tapes distracted me from my attempts at meditation. I could understand the purpose of the tapes— they provided a model of "proper" Naikan, offered hope, suggested topics for the client's self-analysis, broke up the long periods of silence; in addition, they could be purchased later so as to encourage posttreatment continuity during the phase in which the client was advised to practice daily Naikan in his home. Yet I found the sometimes tearful and guilt-filled confessions difficult to endure.

At this time my resistance to the introspection took the form that I had somehow balanced the receiving and giving in some relationships and periods and so had forgotten them; in other words, I had been able to achieve a comfortable closure in some relationships and thus had been able to dismiss them from memory.

But the feelings of gratitude toward others began to build as early as this first morning. I noticed my voice becoming softer, even more distant, like the voices of those around me.

The screen a few inches from my face symbolized well the sense of being closed up within myself. I began to realize that as I rehearsed what I would say to the sensei at each of his visits I was repeating over and over a perspective on my personal history that was simplified and slanted in the typical Naikan fashion.

At 2:05 P.M. a song played over the loudspeaker system linking the goddess Kannonsama with the concept of "mother." The old man in a nearby corner was sniffling audibly. During his next mensetsu I overheard him request only milk for his meals during the remainder of his stay. It is not uncommon for clients to decide to fast during Naikan training. During this day I began noticing that I was having optical illusions of movement out of the corner of my eye.

Later in the afternoon a new client arrived and settled quietly into his corner. At six-fifty on Monday evening Yoshimoto's wife conducted the mensetsu interview, the twelfth since my coming. The sensei was away delivering a lecture. Just before this interview I had something of a hallucination in which I saw golden altarpieces projected in the air nearby. Perhaps I was beginning to doze at that time.

On the third day I became aware that my voice was rising in pitch, becoming more childlike. I had some immunity from the full impact of the broadcasts of Naikan tapes because of my limited vocabulary, but the emotion-laden voices and tears had their impact, as when one hears a baby, any baby, cry. During the sixteenth visit after my confession, the sensei asked whether I felt I had been a good or a bad person in one relationship. I had trouble deciding. He pressed: Which was I closest to? He obviously wanted and expected me to say "bad." And I did. Yet the question lingered in my mind like an unpleasant aftertaste. It was too simple. Not good or bad. Both. Westerners, with their decidedly rationalistic approach to existence, have more defenses at their disposal than the Japanese, who strongly emphasize feeling orientations in their social relationships. For us, relationships are complex and motivations are complicated. Was the *act* bad or was *I* bad? Why did my mother take care of me? Love? Social pressure? Obligation? Or simply without thinking, as part of her role?

By the afternoon of the third day my self-analysis was at its deepest. I was remorseful about the periods of wasted energy and unconcern for others. I saw the need for renewed efforts in behalf of those around me. I rededicated myself to such goals. This realization was neither a conversion experience nor a complete adoption of a Naikan view of the world. I could never see social relationships in the simple black-and-white way of Naikan. On the other hand, the commitment I did make was not without some emotional accompaniment. The balance between experiencing and observing is difficult to maintain. I could see men as puppets but also as their own puppeteers. The strings of time allowing for freedom of movement are at first too long. But they gradually grow shorter, and then too short. That night I dreamed of a clock stopping.

On the fourth day I was still somewhat "high" from my new resolve. In my diary I wrote, "People are to be treasured; I've treated them lightly, haughtily." I determined to make an effort to do more than merely listen to people. I resolved to try to treasure their words.

My ability to recollect the past varied considerably from time to time. But as I maintained a condition of attentive readiness I was able to slip into deep concentration when "conditions" were ready.

Each day we were given twenty minutes in which to bathe. We were instructed to do Naikan as we bathed, ate, worked, and prepared to sleep. Perhaps the daily bath has a symbolic cleansing function within this setting. In the absolute, isolated bed-rest regime of Morita therapy the patient is allowed only one bath during the week.

By the end of the fourth day I had begun to drift into fantasies, random thinking, future planning, and mental calculations of various sorts. In the next few days my role as observer dominated my mental activity, and I accomplished only a minimum of Naikan reflection. My thinking was becoming increasingly analytic. Were my memories genuine recollections or events I had been told about later? Why ought a child return favors equally to his parents? Why become stirred up about one's inability to keep his social ledger of years ago balanced? I began to focus my attention on the constant pressure to make me see my past in a prescribed way. In general, I began to react against my initial leaning toward a more Naikanlike world view.

I noted that in limited ritualized contexts even small deviations of behavior on the part of the client tend to be noticeable and stereotyped and are therefore meaningful diagnostic indicators to the experienced therapist. The sensei responded to the emotional outbursts on the tapes and to those of my companions with unruffled acceptance, directing the client on to more and deeper Naikan.

In the early dawn of the fifth day, before Yoshimoto Sensei's thirty-second visit, I sat wondering if Naikan meditation on the topic of one's wife, sweetheart, or children might have more impact on Americans that Naikan on one's mother or employer. Particularly with regard to employers Americans seem to hold a basic distrust of those in power, whereas many Japanese see their direct supervisors as benevolent figures. Of course, the sensei would disagree with my impression that Americans would be less moved than Japanese when reflecting on their mothers. He holds that in any culture the fundamental social relationship is that between mother and child and that therein lies the wellsprings for guilt and gratitude. Perhaps so; one would suspect that a number of ethologists and psychoanalysts would agree with the primacy of such a relationship. And so would I. The only question is whether or not such a relationship is so separated by time as to make Naikan recollection impractical. Apparently, it is not so for the Japanese.

By now, those who had arrived before me had gone, and others had come to do Naikan. I was the senior Naikansha in the room. Now and again I could hear my fellow clients sobbing.

As I delved into my early years I discovered that settings from my childhood are the settings of some of my dreams in recent years, although the dreams are populated by current acquaintances. From my past, I recalled houses, room arrangements, streets, routes to school, and the like, but I was not nearly as adept at digging out specific acts or relationships.

On the evening of the fifth day I turned my mind loose for awhile— perhaps the best way to describe the process of letting go and observing one's mind operate on its own—and it unreeled a purple-and-lavender undulating flower arrangement, then a sequence with loose associations involving my mother and sister. There were occasional visual illusions, both spontaneous and purposefully created. I was becoming increasingly bored. There were small holes that had been made in the screen and wall near where I sat. They represented the boredom, curiosity, and needs for stimulation of those who sat doing Naikan before me.

Except for the periodic visits by the sensei, there is no checking on the client's use of his time. It is for his own benefit that he is doing Naikan. It is assumed that he spends his time wisely in meditation. When he does not, his conscience is likely to bother him. This may prompt him to confess his lax attitude to the sensei and motivate him to do Naikan more diligently after that.

Interestingly, both Naikan and Morita therapies view the roots of neurosis as self-centeredness or selfishness. Directing one's attention toward serving others is the ultimate goal of both forms of Japanese psychotherapy. Therapists of both types would say that they are both individual-focused *and* society-focused. They contend that most forms of Western insight therapy emphasize the individual to such a degree that Western therapists ignore the basic truth that individual satisfactions can be achieved only when a person is committed to the service of others (as therapists themselves are).

Yet with all this analytical thinking, my diary notes on the sixth day read: "I feel weighted down by all the confessed sins I've heard on the tapes as well as my own thought-over wrongs. Sighs, chest pressure. . . ." On the same day I had a couple of psychic experiences. I had a premonition that there would be an earthquake shortly before one actually began. Perhaps I had felt some prequake tremors without awareness. Perhaps the intuitive warning sense that animals seem to have prior to earthquakes can be developed in man, too. Once, when I heard the telephone ring downstairs, I "knew" that it concerned me. This thought was confirmed by the sensei at his next mensetsu, the forty-fourth. When I could no longer concentrate, I sat listening to the sounds of time passing: a dog's bark, crickets chirping, auto horns, footsteps.

On the sixth night my dreams were confused and varied. I dreamed of my family and of my efforts to flee from a crime organization's plan to watch and kill me. I also dreamed of Yoshimoto Sensei asking me, as he did at each mensetsu, what I had been meditating about. There were other dreams. I woke at 1:00 A.M. and had a little difficulty getting back to sleep. As usual we were awakened at 4:50 A.M. on Saturday.

On the morning of the seventh day I looked back with some feeling of accomplishment on the David Reynolds of Monday and Tuesday safely tucked into the past (à la Frankl 1963). I reflected on the thought that this had been a week in which other people had fought, died, made love, gave birth, argued, and so forth while I sat walled off from the world, existing in my inner world of consciousness for much of the time.

After the fifty-second interview, at five-forty on Saturday evening, Yoshimoto sensei asked me if I would like to practice Naikan guidance of others. I replied that I would. After observing the sensei interview one client, I interviewed a second. Then I completed two rounds of all the clients. I felt somewhat flattered and pleased to be permitted this experience, but I also felt an overwhelming sense of responsibility. And listening to the utterances of guilt and sorrow from the clients was oppressive and very painful. Who was I to guide someone in this agonizing inner search? For me, as I bowed before each client, the obeisance symbolized not only my respect for him but also my genuine humility as I prepared to listen to his confession.

At 7:30 A.M. on the eighth day I prepared to leave the Naikan Center. I stood in the doorway of the large upstairs room. In three corners I could see screens set up closing off clients in their meditative worlds. In a small voice I told them good-bye and, using the same words that Yoshimoto Sensei pronounced, admonished them to introspect earnestly: "Sayonara. . . . Shikkari shirabete kudasai" (Good-bye. . . . Please examine yourselves zealously).

The strong glow of gratitude toward others, even strangers, lasted for a few days. I wrote a number of letters to family and friends who meant much to me, thanking them for their contributions to my life. I sent off a number of gifts. The intensity of this feeling state declined over the next few months, but perhaps the effects of adopting a Naikan perspective will never completely disappear. I sincerely hope not. It provided me with another reference point to gain perspective on the element of egocentric individualism in Western man.

NAIKAN IN THE UNITED STATES

In August 1981 the first intensive Naikan retreat in the United States was conducted in San Luis Obispo. It was held in a Shinshu Buddhist church. Eleven Naikansha attended. They included three Japanese, four Japanese-Americans, one Korean, one Chinese American, and two Anglo-Americans. Nearly all were in their late twenties and thirties. Most were therapists or religious professionals. Four women participated.

The author planned the retreat schedule, conducted mensetsu, and served meals, with some assistance. Only one Naikansha spoke Japanese exclusively and two others spoke Japanese occasionally during mensetsu.

The week of Naikan began on Sunday morning and ended Saturday afternoon. The typical daily schedule was as follows:

5:30 A.M.	Lights on
5:30–6:15	Wash up and clean area
6:15–6:30	Chanting
6:30	Naikan sitting
6:45	Breakfast while Naikan continues
12 noon	Lunch while Naikan continues
12:30–1 P.M.	Group meeting
1:00	Naikan sitting
6:00	Dinner while Naikan continues
6:30–7:15	Kinhin walking while Naikan continues
7:15	Naikan sitting
9:00	Chanting
9:20	Lights out

On the first day an orientation meeting was held and a videotape of Naikan practice in Japan was shown. On the last day an extended group meeting allowed the participants to share verbally their Naikan experiences. Questionnaires were administered during these meetings.

Prior to the retreat nearly every Naikansha had read at least one article about Naikan. About half of the participants came through the encouragement of an acquaintance. They gave as their reasons for coming either self-discovery or curiosity about Naikan practice. They reported either no expectations about this meditative technique or the expectation of personal growth.

Following the week of intensive Naikan all reported the experience to have been helpful (though the reasons varied), and they responded that they would "recommend Naikan to others." All but one reported that they had changed their view of themselves as a result of the week's effort and that they intended to do daily Naikan in the future. About half indicated their desire to do intensive Naikan again.

Overall, the retreat was extremely successful. It can be argued that the participants were not representative Westerners—nine of the eleven were of Asian background, and the remaining two had shown previous interest in Eastern meditation. Yet the degree of Naikan's impact appeared to be unrelated to the degree of Westernization of the Naikansha. The two Caucasians were strongly affected by their experience, and the greatest resistance to this form of self-reflection was exhibited by a Japanese national and a Japanese-American.

It is too early to assess the relative potential of Naikan in the West. However, the arguments that it cannot be practiced in the West at all or that it cannot have any positive influence on Westerners must now be abandoned. It was and it did.

Naikan therapy as an adjunct mode in outpatient psychotherapy is just beginning in the United States. It is currently being practiced at the ToDo Institute in Los Angeles and at the Health Center Pacific on Maui. On an outpatient basis Naikan may be carried out by means of a journal. Ordinarily clients write a page daily following the nichijo (daily) Naikan themes. That is, in the morning for at least thirty minutes the clients reflect on a particular person and time period from the past in sequence up to the present. In the evening they reflect for another thirty minutes on what was received from others, returned to them, and what troubles were caused to others during that day. The journal is turned in at the weekly sessions for the therapist's comments. Sometimes the client is invited to read aloud the most significant entries from the week's journal.

At this juncture outpatient Naikan appears to be appropriate for clients with difficulties in love relationships, histories of victimization with subsequent adoption of a generalized victim role, parental and marital discord, some sorts of unemployment and job problems, and desires to deepen personal or spiritual growth. This list will undoubtedly expand after there is more clinical experience with the method.

To date, outpatient Naikan appears not to have caused harm to anyone. Some clients resist it strongly and some refuse it altogether. In such cases one can often find clear usefulness to the client in maintaining the existing perspective on the past.

Naikan seems to work very well in conjunction with Morita therapy (Reynolds, 1981a, 1981b) and with various forms of pastoral counseling. At this point in time little is known about the practical fit of Naikan as an adjunct therapy with psychoanalysis, behavior therapies, logotherapy, or other treatment modes.

Appendix A

Tables

Table 1 1977 Nara Center Naikansha

A. Age and Sex	Age	N	% of Males	% of Total
Males	19 and younger	151	19.4	13.2
	20–29	236	30.3	20.6
	30–39	212	27.2	18.5
	40–49	102	13.1	8.9
	50–59	44	5.7	3.8
	60 and older	33	4.2	2.9
	Total	778	99.9%	68%
		N	% of Females	% of Total
Females	19 and younger	57	15.6	5.0
	20–29	116	31.8	10.1
	30–39	76	20.8	6.6
	40–49	67	18.4	5.9
	50–59	23	6.3	2.0
	60 and older	26	7.1	2.3
	Total	365	100%	32%
Both-sex Totals		1,143		99.8%

B. Occupation	N	%
Professional (physician, psychologist, social worker, therapist)	13	1.9
Educator, teacher	53	4.6
Office worker	399	34.9
Housewife	60	5.2
Unmarried daughter helping with housework	17	1.5
Self-employed, sales, service	77	6.7
Student	259	22.7
Hospital employee	40	3.5
Farmworker	14	1.2
Cook	11	1.0
None (includes some housewives)	129	11.3
Other (includes prison employees)	16	1.4
Unknown, unclear	55	4.8
Total	1,143	99.9%

149

Table 2   NARA NAIKAN KENSHUJO REGISTERED NAIKANSHA, 1955 THROUGH 1959 (5 YEARS)

Age	Males	%	Females	%	Totals	%
19 and younger	38	18.3	3	13.0	41	17.7
20–29 years	107	51.4	8	34.8	115	49.8
30–39 years	24	11.5	4	17.4	28	12.1
40–49 years	15	7.2	1	4.3	16	6.9
50–59 years	9	4.3	6	26.1	15	6.5
60 and older	6	2.9	1	4.3	7	3.0
Age unknown	9	4.3	0	0	9	3.9
Total	208		23		231	

Table 3   NAIKAN DEPTH

No rating	Returned home without doing Naikan; don't recall.
0	Doesn't even like to talk with therapist.
1	Thinks only of being sent by family.
2	Sits only because he can't avoid the situation.
3	Talks some with the therapist.
4	Exhibits some, though meager, Naikan.
5	Shows some motivation. Naikan is not useless.
6	Enthusiastic. Some are worthy of tape recording.
7	Highly enthusiastic (good effort). Definitely should tape-record. A true Naikansha.
8	Superior enthusiasm. An excellent Naikansha.
9	Rarely seen, a model Naikansha.
10	Supreme Naikansha. No one rated such yet.

Appendix A

Table 4   DEPTH OF NAIKAN, NARA NAIKAN CENTER, 1966–74

Age (Years)	0–2 Rating (%) (Shallow Naikan)	7–9 Rating (%) (Deep Naikan)
19 and younger	29.5	1.7
20–29	18.9	5.2
30–39	14.0	10.9
40–49	12.4	15.4
50–59	14.2	11.8
60 and older	35.5	7.3
All males	21.7	5.7
All females	17.4	9.4
Totals (males and females)	20.3	6.9

SOURCE: R. Takeda, personal communication.

Table 5   RECIDIVISM AND NAIKAN

Prison and Year	Naikan	Released	Reimprisoned	% Reimprisoned
Tottori, 1958–59	Yes (experimental)	243	54	22.2
	No (control group)	895	490	54.7
Tokushima, 1959–62	Yes	629	191	30.4
	No	2,229	1,340	60.1
Miyazaki, 1960–61	Yes	204	29	14.4
	No	813	653	80.3
Matsuyama, 1961–63	Yes	148	9	6.1
	No	1,005	171	17.0
Hiroshima, 1960–64	Yes	492	112	22.8
	No	1,717	586	33.1
Okinawa, 1961–68	Yes	493	106	21.5
	No	No data	No data	85.0
Kokura, 1958–59	Yes	135	5	3.7
	No	662	85	12.8

SOURCE: adapted from Takeda 1975

151

Table 6 Age Group, by Setting

	Nara N	(%)	Senkobo N	(%)	Meguro N	(%)	Gasshoen N	(%)	Yoyogi N	(%)	Ibusuki N	(%)
10–19 years	71	(21.1)	43	(48.9)	1	(7.7)	2	(2.0)	2	(6.7)	4	(11.8)
20–29	77	(22.8)	17	(19.3)	4	(30.8)	13	(13.1)	3	(10.0)	3	(8.8)
30–39	80	(23.7)	10	(11.4)	1	(7.7)	11	(11.1)	6	(20.0)	4	(11.8)
40–49	55	(16.3)	15	(17.0)	3	(23.1)	17	(17.2)	9	(30.0)	19	(55.9)
50–59	38	(11.3)	3	(3.4)	3	(23.1)	17	(17.2)	4	(13.3)	2	(5.9)
60 and older	16	(4.7)	0	(0)	1	(7.7)	39	(39.4)	6	(20.0)	2	(5.9)
Mean age (years)	33.5		25.7		40.2		52.2		45.2		40.1	
Range (years)	11–80		11–61		17–75		15–86		11–70		13–73	

Table 7 Sex, by Setting

	Nara N	(%)	Senkobo N	(%)	Meguro N	(%)	Gasshoen N	(%)	Yoyogi N	(%)	Ibusuki N	(%)
Male	204	(60.5)	59	(67.0)	5	(38.5)	35	(35.0)	12	(40.0)	28	(80.0)
Female	133	(39.5)	29	(33.0)	8	(61.5)	65	(65.0)	18	(60.0)	7	(20.0)

Table 8 OCCUPATION, BY SETTING

	Nara N	Nara (%)	Senkobo N	Senkobo (%)	Meguro N	Meguro (%)	Gasshoen N	Gasshoen (%)	Yoyogi N	Yoyogi (%)	Ibusuki N	Ibusuki (%)
Professional therapist	7	(2.1)	0	(0)	0	(0)	0	(0)	0	(0)	0	(0)
Educator	20	(6.0)	4	(4.5)	1	(7.7)	2	(2.0)	1	(3.3)	1	(2.9)
Office worker, manager	85	(25.3)	19	(21.6)	3	(23.1)	17	(17.3)	8	(26.7)	5	(14.7)
Housewife, househelper	28	(8.3)	5	(5.7)	2	(15.4)	11	(11.2)	5	(16.7)	0	(0)
Student	82	(24.4)	45	(51.1)	2	(15.4)	2	(2.0)	2	(6.7)	4	(11.8)
Hospital employee	23	(6.8)	1	(1.1)	0	(0)	0	(0)	0	(0)	0	(0)
Farmer	4	(1.2)	0	(0)	1	(7.7)	26	(26.5)	0	(0)	3	(8.8)
Other	45	(13.4)	7	(8.0)	2	(15.4)	15	(15.3)	9	(30.0)	11	(32.4)
None, unemployed, retired	42	(12.5)	7	(8.0)	2	(15.4)	25	(25.5)	5	(16.7)	10	(29.4)

Table 9 RELIGION, BY SETTING

	Nara N	Nara (%)	Senkobo N	Senkobo (%)	Meguro N	Meguro (%)	Gasshoen N	Gasshoen (%)	Yoyogi N	Yoyogi (%)	Ibusuki N	Ibusuki (%)
Jodo Shinshu	53	(21.5)	20	(32.8)	1	(8.3)	73	(83.0)	5	(22.7)	11	(32.4)
Zen	9	(3.6)	2	(3.3)	1	(8.3)	6	(6.8)	1	(4.5)	0	(0)
Buddhist, other	61	(24.7)	20	(32.8)	2	(16.7)	6	(6.8)	3	(13.6)	5	(14.7)
Christian	13	(5.3)	1	(1.6)	1	(8.3)	0	(0)	2	(9.1)	0	(0)
G.L.A.	31	(12.6)	5	(8.2)	0	(0)	0	(0)	4	(18.2)	0	(0)
New sect	9	(3.6)	0	(0)	1	(8.3)	1	(1.1)	2	(9.1)	4	(11.8)
Other	7	(2.8)	4	(6.6)	0	(0)	0	(0)	0	(0)	3	(8.8)
None	64	(25.9)	9	(14.8)	6	(50.0)	2	(2.3)	5	(22.7)	11	(32.4)

Table 10 RESIDENCE, BY SETTING

	Nara N	Nara (%)	Senkobo N	Senkobo (%)	Meguro N	Meguro (%)	Gasshoen N	Gasshoen (%)	Yoyogi N	Yoyogi (%)	Ibusuki N	Ibusuki (%)
City	294	(87.8)	65	(75.6)	9	(69.2)	55	(55.0)	28	(93.3)	20	(57.1)
Other (town, village)	41	(12.2)	21	(24.4)	4	(30.8)	45	(45.0)	2	(6.7)	15	(42.9)

Table 11 HOW CLIENT LEARNED OF NAIKAN, BY SETTING

	Nara N	Nara (%)	Senkobo N	Senkobo (%)	Meguro N	Meguro (%)	Gasshoen N	Gasshoen (%)	Yoyogi N	Yoyogi (%)	Ibusuki N	Ibusuki (%)
Book	62	(18.7)	20	(25.0)	4	(30.8)	2	(2.2)	4	(13.3)	3	(8.8)
Friend	55	(16.6)	7	(8.8)	2	(15.4)	25	(27.5)	3	(10.0)	15	(44.1)
Family	48	(14.5)	7	(8.8)	2	(15.4)	24	(26.4)	10	(33.3)	4	(11.8)
Professional therapist	112	(33.7)	4	(5.0)	4	(30.8)	3	(3.3)	0	(0)	12	(35.3)
Teacher	38	(11.4)	29	(36.3)	1	(7.7)	0	(0)	0	(0)	0	(0)
Religious professional	5	(1.5)	3	(3.8)	0	(0)	36	(39.6)	11	(36.7)	0	(0)
Other	12	(4.5)	10	(12.5)	0	(0)	1	(1.1)	2	(6.7)	0	(0)

Table 12 Presenting Problem, by Setting

	Nara N	(%)	Senkobo N	(%)	Meguro N	(%)	Gasshoen N	(%)	Yoyogi N	(%)	Ibusuki N	(%)
Psychiatric diagnosis	43	(13.1)	4	(4.8)	4	(30.8)	7	(7.4)	1	(3.6)	2	(5.7)
Addiction	4	(1.2)	2	(2.4)	0	(0)	0	(0)	1	(3.6)	10	(28.6)
Social problem	120	(36.5)	48	(57.8)	3	(23.1)	33	(34.7)	4	(14.3)	1	(2.9)
Self-development,												
Self-discovery, religion	100	(30.4)	15	(18.1)	3	(23.1)	24	(25.3)	16	(57.1)	15	(42.9)
Training, sent by company	32	(9.7)	8	(9.6)	0	(0)	0	(0)	0	(0)	0	(0)
Illness	13	(4.0)	0	(0)	2	(15.4)	18	(18.9)	2	(7.1)	0	(0)
Other	17	(5.2)	6	(7.2)	1	(7.7)	13	(15.8)	4	(14.2)	7	(20.0)

Table 13 Expected Results, by Setting

	Nara N	(%)	Senkobo N	(%)	Meguro N	(%)	Gasshoen N	(%)	Yoyogi N	(%)	Ibusuki N	(%)
Self-oriented	253	(80.6)	63	(79.7)	10	(83.3)	55	(63.2)	20	(74.1)	21	(61.8)
Do Naikan	12	(3.8)	10	(12.7)	0	(0)	7	(8.0)	0	(0)	3	(8.8)
Cure	13	(4.1)	0	(0)	1	(8.3)	5	(5.7)	0	(0)	8	(23.5)
Other-oriented	31	(9.9)	6	(7.6)	1	(8.3)	12	(13.8)	4	(14.8)	2	(5.9)
Religious	2	(0.6)	0	(0)	0	(0)	8	(9.2)	1	(3.7)	0	(0)
Other	3	(1.0)	0	(0)	0	(0)	0	(0)	2	(7.4)	0	(0)

Table 14 THERAPISTS' RESPONSES

	Nara	Gasshoen	Senkobo	Meguro	Minami Toyota	Ibusuki
1. When began as therapist	1937	1974	—	1971	1976	1975
2. Maximum total patients treated directly by a therapist	50,000–60,000	1,700	?	502	103	268
3. Patients treated, 1977	1,143	450	267	125	60	80
4. By age: male/female	1977	Total	1977	Total	Total	Total
19 and younger	151/57	100/100	72/44	22/7	2/2	5/11
20–29	236/116	100/200	33/14	150/50	12/1	29/12
30–39	212/76	100/300	24/6	150/50	34/0	55/6
40–49	102/67	150/250	14/4	39/10	40/0	97/6
50–59	44/23	50/150	5/3	15/5	8/0	32/3
60 and older	33/26	50/150	3/2	3/1	4/0	12/0
?	0/0	0/0	29/14	0/0	0/0	0/0
% males/females	68/32	34/66	67/33	75/25	97/3	86/14
5. Presenting problem	Est. %	Est. %	Est. %	Est. %	Est. %	Est. %
a. Psychosis	5	4	8	4	0	5
b. Neurosis	5	4	12	40	1	1
c. Addiction	5	2	8	1	99	84
d. Delinquency	9	8	49	2	0	2
e. Family problem	5	39	4	7	0	1
f. Work problem	1	16	3	4	0	0
g. School problem	2	4	1	4	0	0
h. Love problem	1	4	1	5	0	0

Appendix A

	10/40/50 1977 %	20/70/10 Total est. %	10/80/10 1977 %	20/50/30 Total est. %	5/35/60 Total est. %	? Total est. %
i. Self-development	9	6	4	20	0	4
j. Religious experience	18	7	2	2	0	0
k. Company training program	5	6	8	10	0	1
l. Other	35	0	0	0	0	2
Social Status (est. %)						
Upper/mid/lower	10/40/50	20/70/10	10/80/10	20/50/30	5/35/60	?
Naikansha occupation	1977 %	Total est. %	1977 %	Total est. %	Total est. %	Total est. %
Student	23	14	45	18	2	4
Farmers	1	17	4	?	?	?
White-collar workers	35	14	22	36	19	16
Merchants	7	5	4	16	10	2
Housewives	5	45	15	10	1	4
Unemployed, retired	11	3	4	6	35	12
Other	4	0	4	2	19	46
Unclear, unknown	5	0	0	6	15	14
Hospital employees	3	0	0	0	0	0
Therapists	1	0	1	0	0	0
Educators	5	3	4	6	0	2
Longest period of Naikan	3 weeks	1 week	1 month	1 month	1 week	2 weeks
Shortest period of Naikan	1 hour	3 days	3 days	½ day	1 day	1 day
Average period of Naikan	1 week	1 week	7–10 days	1 week	6.8 days	8.5 days
Results(%)						
Excellent	40	53	100	8	19	7
Good	20	27	0	24	49	23
Fair	20	13	0	56	18	38
Poor	0	0	0	8	0	16
Stopped before completion	20	1	0	0	13	6
Unclear	0	7	0	4	0	0

Table 14 *(cont.)*

	Nara	Gasshoen	Senkobo	Meguro	Minami Toyota	Ibusuki
Percentage of Naikansha who have been to another Naikan facility	1	1	6	56	0	0
Percentage of Naikansha who come from same prefecture as this Naikan facility	1	50	20	60	95	90
How did Naikansha learn about this facility?	Est. %	Est. %	Est. %	Est. %	Est. %	Est. %
Newspaper	0	8	2	4	0	0
Book	10	8	3	25	12	13
Family	10	63	21	21	19	?
Company	20	8	12	17	17	20
Friend	5	8	15	8	14	20
Doctor	20	1	3	13	21	20
Teacher	30	4	40	13	0	27
Legal authority	0	0	1	0	0	0
Unclear	0	0	0	0	0	0
Other	5	0	0	0	0	0
Psychological or health Counselor	1	0	3	0	18	0

Table 15 Comparison of Questionnaire Sample and Therapists' Estimates of Naikansha, by Age Group

	Nara		Gasshoen		Senkobo		Meguro		Ibusuki	
	Estimate(%)	Sample(%)	Estimate(%)	Sample(%)	Estimate(%)	Sample(%)	Estimate(%)	Sample(%)	Estimate(%)	Sample(%)
10–19 years	18.2	21.1	11.8	2.8	43.4	49.4	5.8	7.7	6.0	11.4
20–29	30.8	22.8	17.6	13.1	17.6	18.4	39.8	30.8	15.3	8.6
30–39	25.2	23.7	23.5	11.1	11.2	11.5	39.8	7.7	22.8	11.4
40–49	14.8	16.3	23.5	17.2	6.7	17.2	9.8	23.1	38.4	57.1
50–59	5.9	11.3	11.8	17.2	3.0	3.4	4.0	23.1	13.1	5.7
60 and older	5.1	4.7	11.8	39.4	1.9	0	.8	7.7	4.5	5.7
Unknown	0	0	0	0	16.1	0	0	0	0	0

Table 16 Comparison of Questionnaire Sample and Therapists' Estimate of Naikansha, by Sex

	Nara		Gasshoen		Senkobo		Meguro		Ibusuki	
	Estimate(%)	Sample(%)	Estimate(%)	Sample(%)	Estimate(%)	Sample(%)	Estimate(%)	Sample(%)	Estimate(%)	Sample(%)
Male	68	60.5	34	35.0	67	67.0	75	38.5	86	80
Female	32	39.5	66	65.0	33	33.0	25	61.5	14	20

159

Appendix B

Back-Translated Questionnaire
for Clients

Questionnaire for Naikansha
(For Naikansha from July 1 to September 30, 1978)

Naikan facility _____ Name _____ Date _____

Occupation _____ Age _____ Religion _____

Sex _____ Number of older brothers _____

Number of older sisters _____ Number of younger brothers _____

Number of younger sisters _____ Father's occupation _____

Father's age _____ Mother's age _____

Address _____

When did you first learn about Naikan? _____

How did you learn about it? _____

Were you advised/encouraged by someone to come? _____

How did you select this facility? _____

Do you know others who have done Naikan? _____ How many? _____

Have you read books and magazines about Naikan? _____

How many? _____

Does anyone know that you have come here? _____ Who? _____

Are there people you don't want to know about your coming here? _____

Who? _____

What prompted you to do Naikan? _____

What positive results do you think will come after doing Naikan? _____

Looking back on yourself from the present, assign the proper number in the box next to the following questions:

    1. Were you warm and kind to other people? □

    2. Did you follow through on others' advice? □

    3. Were you mature and honest? □

    4. Did you take responsibility and act? □

    5. Did you forgive others' mistakes and failures? □

        1. Certainly

        2. Perhaps

        3. Neither yes nor no

        4. Perhaps not

        5. Absolutely not

Appendix B

What do you think about the next set of opinions?
Put a number in the box next to the following:
1. People think only of themselves. □
2. No one cares about anyone else. □
3. Because people are self-seeking you can't trust them. □
4. Most people, deep down, dislike helping others. □
5. The world is a cold place. □

1. That is certainly true
2. Perhaps it is so
3. One can't say yes or no
4. It's probably not so
5. It is never so

Dr. David Reynolds, a professor at the University of Southern California, is conducting this research. Please cooperate. Please return by the end of September.

Naikan Training Center
Yoshimoto Ishin, Director

161

Appendix C

Back-Translated Questionnaire
for Therapists

Questionnaire about Naikan Therapy

Name _____ Date _____ Place/Setting _____
When did you first learn about Naikan therapy? _____
When did you become a Naikansha client? _____
    Where was that? _____
    First time _____ Date _____ Place _____
    Second time _____
    Third time _____

When did you first become a Naikan therapist? _____
Up to the present how many Naikansha have you treated? _____
In 1977 how many Naikan clients did you treat? _____
    A. Among them, how many were

	Male	Female		Male	Female
19 and younger	____	____	40–49	____	____
20–29	____	____	50–59	____	____
30–39	____	____	60 and older	____	____

    B. What was their motivation in doing Naikan?
        Psychosis _____
        Neurosis _____
        Addiction (alcoholism, other) _____
        Delinquency _____
        Social problems _____
            Family problems _____ School problems _____
            Work problems _____ Love problems _____
        Self-discovery _____
        Religious purpose _____
        Sent by company _____
        Other _____
    C. Social status: upper _____% middle _____% lower _____%
    D. School and work history
        Junior high student _____   Merchant _____
        High school student _____   Housewife _____
        College prep school student _____   Unemployed _____
        Educator _____   Other _____
        Civil servant _____   Unclear _____
        Company worker _____
    E. How long did these people do Naikan?
        Longest case _____ Shortest case _____

F. About how much does it cost for a single person to do one day of Naikan? _____

How do they pay?
National health insurance _____
Union health insurance _____
Group health insurance _____
Other health insurance _____
Own funds _____
What happens with people who cannot pay? _____

G. What about the results of Naikan? _____
Extremely good _____
Good _____
Average _____
Poor _____
Stopped without completing _____
Unclear _____
Total _____

H. What percentage do not do Naikan voluntarily? _____

I. What therapies did the clients receive before Naikan? _____
Morita therapy _____   Autogenic training _____
Hypnosis _____   Seiza _____
Behavior therapy _____ Other (specify) _____
Zazen _____   None _____
Individual therapy _____

J. How many clients came only to your Naikan setting and how many had been to other Naikan settings also? _____

K. What percentage of your clients came from within your ken (prefecture)? _____

L. Who introduced them to Naikan?
Newspaper _____   Doctor _____
Book _____   Educator _____
Family _____   Prison official _____
Company _____   Unclear _____
Friend _____   Other _____
Counselor _____

Questions about your Naikan setting

A. What are its unique features? _____

B. How is it doing financially? _____

C. If there is any difference between the way you did Naikan at first and the way you do it now, please describe. _____

D. If you use other therapies also describe how they are carried out with Naikan. _____

E. In the practice of Naikan what are the troublesome areas? _____
_____

F. In the practice of Naikan what are the most satisfying points? ____
_____

G. Do you maintain contact after intensive Naikan (through, for example, magazines, group meetings, letters, etc.)? _____

Questionnaire for Therapists

Therapists' opinion
  A. Naikan is

	Yes	No		Yes	No
Psychotherapy	___	___	Self-development	___	___
Religion	___	___	Other	___	___
Mental-spiritual education	___	___			

  B. In your experience what are the problems most easily cured by Naikan? _____
  C. What are the problems most difficult to cure? _____
  D. Are there problems absolutely incurable by Naikan? _____
     What are they? _____
  E. Do you think Naikan is useful for Westerners?
     Yes _____   No _____
     To some degree _____   Why or why not? _____
  F. Do you think Naikan is useful for modern Japanese youth?
     Yes _____   No _____
     To some degree _____   Why or why not? _____
  G. In order to become a therapist what personality features and training are necessary? _____
  H. What do you think of the future of your Naikan facility? _____
  I. What do you think of the future of Naikan therapy? _____
  J. Please write anything else that will help me understand your Naikan facility. _____

Dr. David Reynolds, a professor at the University of Southern California is conducting this research. Please cooperate. Please return this questionnaire by the end of September.

Nara Training Center
Yoshimoto Ishin, Director

Bibliography

Befu, Harumi. 1974. Gift-giving in a modernizing Japan. In Lebra, T., and Lebra, W., eds., *Japanese Culture and Behavior*. Honolulu: University Press of Hawaii.

———. 1977. The group model of Japanese society. Paper presented at the Meetings of the American Anthropological Association, Houston.

Behavior Today. 1979. *10* (3):7.

Benedict, Ruth. 1946. *The Chrysanthemum and the Sword*. New York: Houghton Mifflin.

Boisen, A. T. 1936. *The Exploration of the Inner World*. New York: Harper.

Caudill, William. 1959. The cultural context of Japanese psychiatry. In Opler, Marvin, ed., *Culture and Mental Health*. New York: Macmillan.

DeVos, George A. 1973. *Socialization for Achievement*. Berkeley: University of California Press.

———. 1980. Afterword. In Reynolds, David K., *The Quiet Therapies*. Honolulu: University Press of Hawaii.

Doi, Takeo. 1973a. Omote and ura. *Journal of Nervous and Mental Disease*, *157*(4):258–61.

———. 1973b. *The Anatomy of Dependence*. Translated by John Bester. Tokyo: Kodansha.

Ekman, Paul. 1975. Face muscles talk every language. *Psychology Today*, September, 35–39.

Feifel, Herman, ed. 1977. *New Meanings of Death*. New York: McGraw-Hill.

Festinger, L. 1964. *Conflict, Decision, and Dissonance*. Stanford: Stanford University Press.

Frank, Jerome D. 1961. *Persuasion and Healing*. Baltimore: Johns Hopkins University Press.

Frankl, Viktor E. 1963. *Man's Search for Meaning*. New York: Washington Square Press.

Freud, Sigmund. 1933. *New Introductory Lectures on Psychoanalysis*. Translated by W. J. H. Sprott. New York: Norton.

Gouldner, Alvin W. 1960. The norm of reciprocity: a preliminary statement. *American Sociological Review*, 25:161–78.

Homans, George C. 1961. *Social Behavior: Its Elementary Forms*. New York: Harcourt Brace and World.

Iga, Mamoru. 1968. Japanese adolescent suicide and social structure. In Schneidman, E. S., ed., *Essays in Self-Destruction*. New York: Science House.

Ishida, Rokuro. 1969. Naikan analysis. *Psychologia*, *12*:81–92.

165

———. 1972. Naikan bunseki ryoho. In Okumura, N., et al., eds., *Naikan Therapy*. Tokyo: Igaku Shoin.

Jourard, Sidney M. 1964. *The Transparent Self*. Princeton, N.J.: Van Nostrand.

Kato, Masaaki. 1969. Naikan kyoiku zakkan. In Yoshimoto, Ishin, ed., *Kyosei to Naikan*. Nara: Naikan Kenshujo.

Kiefer, Christie W. 1970. *Personality and Social Change in a Japanese danchi*. Ph.D. diss. Berkeley: University of California.

Kishioka, Hiroshi. 1978. Naikan ni taisuru teiko ni tsuite. In *Proceedings of the First Naikan Conference*. Nara: Naikan Kenshujo.

Kitsuse, John I. 1965. Moral treatment and reformation of inmates in Japanese prisons. *Psychologia*, 8:9–23.

———. 1968. A method of reform in Japanese prisons. In Schneps, Maurice, and Coox, Alvin, eds., *The Japanese Image*, 2:1–7.

Kodani, Hirumi. 1969. The basic character of neurosis and its cure. *Naikan*, 3:32–50.

Kusunoki, Masami. 1976. *Kokoro no Tanken*. Tokyo: Togensha.

———. 1978. Shukyo to shite no Naikanho. *Kiyo*, 13:89–101.

———. 1980. Naikanho no giho ni tsuite kangaeru. In *Proceedings of the Third Naikan Conference*. Tokyo: Naikan Association.

Lebra, Takie S. 1974. Reciprocity and the assymetric principle: an analytic reappraisal of the Japanese concept of *on*. In Lebra, T., and Lebra, W., eds., *Japanese Culture and Behavior*. Honolulu: University Press of Hawaii.

———. 1976. *Japanese Patterns of Behavior*. Honolulu: University Press of Hawaii.

London, Perry. 1964. *The Modes and Morals of Psychotherapy*. New York: Holt, Rinehart and Winston.

Mead, George H. 1913. The social self. *Journal of Philosophy, Psychology and Scientific Methods*, 10:374–80.

Miki, Yoshihiko [Sogi, Yoshihiko]. 1967. *Shinri Ryoho to shite no Naikanho Hitotsu Kenkyu*. Ph.D. diss., Osaka University. Nara: Naikan Kenshujo.

Miki, Yoshihiko. 1972a. The process of attitude change in delinquent youth. In Okumura, N., et al., eds., *Naikan Ryoho*. Tokyo: Igaku Shoin.

———. 1972b. Basic results of Naikan according to psychological tests. In Okumura, N., et al., eds., *Naikan Ryoho*. Tokyo: Igaku Shoin.

———. 1978. *Naikan Ryoho Nyumon*. Osaka: Sogensha.

———. N.d. Shonensei no Naikan no jirei kenkyu. In Yoshimoto, Ishin, ed., *Kyosei to Naikan*. Nara: Naikan Kenshujo.

Mowrer, O. H. 1961. *The Crisis in Psychiatry and Religion*. Princeton, N.J.: Van Nostrand.

———. 1964. *The New Group Therapy*. Princeton, N.J.: Van Nostrand.

Murase, Takao. 1972. Counselor-client relation in Naikan. Twentieth International Congress of Psychology, *Abstracts*. Tokyo.

———. 1974. Naikan therapy. In Lebra, T., and Lebra, W., eds., *Japanese Culture and Behavior*. Honolulu: University Press of Hawaii.

Murase, Takao, and Johnson, F. 1973. Naikan, Morita and Western psychotherapy: a comparison. Paper presented at the American Psychiatric Association Meetings, Honolulu.

Bibliography

Murase, Takao, and Reynolds, David. N.d. *Naikan Therapy*. Pamphlet. Nara: Naikan Training Center.

Nakamura, Hajime. 1964. In Weiner, P., ed., *Ways of Thinking of Eastern Peoples*. Honolulu: University Press of Hawaii.

Nakane, Chie. 1972. *Japanese Society*. Berkeley: University of California Press.

Narita, Toshio. 1978. Kyosei Shisetsu ni Okeru Naikanho no Riyo Jokyo. In *Proceedings of the First Naikan Conference*. Nara: Naikan Kenshujo.

Okawa, Shigeyuki, and Takemoto, Ryuyo. 1978. Changes in blood pressure and pulse in intensive Naikan. In *Proceedings of the First Naikan Conference*. Nara: Naikan Kenshujo.

Okumura, Nikichi; Sato, Koji; and Yamamoto, Haruo, eds. 1972. *Naikan Therapy*. Tokyo: Igaku Shoin.

Reynolds, David K. 1972. What is man? *Seishin Ryoho Kenkyu Zasshi*, 4(1):51–54.

———. 1976. *Morita Psychotherapy*. Berkeley: University of California Press.

———. 1977. Naikan therapy—an experiential view. *International Journal of Social Psychiatry*, 23(4):252–64.

———. 1978. The introduction of Japanese therapies into America. In *Proceedings of the First Naikan Conference*. Nara: Naikan Kenshujo.

———. 1980. *The Quiet Therapies*. Honolulu: University Press of Hawaii.

———. 1981a. Naikan therapy. In Corsini, Raymond, ed. *Handbook of Innovative Psychotherapies*, New York: John Wiley.

———. 1981b. Morita therapy. In Corsini, Raymond, ed. *Handbook of Innovative Psychotherapies*. New York: John Wiley.

Reynolds, David K., and Farberow, Norman L. 1976. *Suicide: Inside and Out*. Berkeley: University of California Press.

Reynolds, David K., and Kiefer, Christie W. 1977. Cultural adaptability as an attribute of therapies: the case of Morita psychotherapy. *Culture, Medicine, and Psychiatry*. 1:395–412.

Reynolds, David K., and Yamamoto, Joe. 1973. Morita psychotherapy in Japan. *Current Psychiatric Therapies*, 13:219–27.

Saunders, E. Dale. 1964. *Buddhism in Japan*. Philadelphia: University of Pennsylvania Press.

Shinfuku, Naotake. 1971. Foreword. In Yoshimoto, Ishin, ed., *Nayami no Kaiketsu Ho*. Nara: Naikan Kenshujo.

Soskin, William F., and John, Vera P. 1963. The study of spontaneous talk. In Barker, Roger G., ed., *The Stream of Behavior*. New York: Appleton-Century-Crofts.

Suzuki, D. T. 1970. *Shin Buddhism*. New York: Harper and Row.

Tada, Y., and Miki, Y. 1972. Naikan no Kekka, 1 and 2. In Okumura, N., et al., eds., *Naikan Ryoho*. Tokyo: Igaku Shoin.

Takeda, Ryuji. 1971. The participation of private citizens in crime prevention. *UNAFEI Resources Materials Series*, no. 2.

———. 1975. Table: Recidivism and setting of prisoners who did Naikan. In Yoshimoto, Ishin, *Naikanho*. Nara: Naikan Kenshujo.

———. 1977. Tables: Naikan depth by age and sex, and Nara Naikansha by year and sex. In Yoshimoto, Ishin, *Naikan no Michi*. Nara: Naikan Kenshujo.

————. 1978. Consciousness of prison employees regarding Naikan. In *Proceedings of the First Naikan Gakkai*. Nara: Naikan Kenshujo.

Takemoto, Ryoyo. 1978. Naikan to igaku. In Yoshimoto, Ishin, ed., *Naikan to Seishin Eisei*. Nara: Naikan Kenshujo.

Takeuchi, Katashi. 1965. On "Naikan." *Psychologia, 8*:2–8.

————. 1972. Rogers and Karen Horney Comparisons. In Okumura, N., et al., eds., *Naikan Ryoho*. Tokyo: Igaku Shoin.

Tamura, Yoshiro, ed. 1960. *Living Buddhism in Japan*. Tokyo: International Institute for the Study of Religions.

Yamamoto, Haruo. 1972a. Genri sosetsu. In Okumura, N., et al., eds., *Naikan Ryoho*. Tokyo: Igaku Shoin.

————. 1972b. Naikan ni taisuru hihan. In Okumura, N., et al., eds., *Naikan Ryoho*. Igaku Shoin.

Yamamoto, Tatsuro. 1964. Recent studies in Japanese national character. In Northrop, F. S. C., and Livingston, Helen, eds., *Cross-Cultural Understanding*. New York: Harper and Row.

Yanagida, Kakusei. 1980. Kaisetsu no kozo to Naikan. In *Proceedings of the Third Naikan Conference*. Tokyo: Naikan Association.

Yokoyama, Shigeo. 1978. Followup of intensive Naikan clients. In *Proceedings of the First Naikan Gakki*. Nara: Naikan Kenshujo.

Yoshimoto, Inobu. 1958. *Self-Reflection Will Guide You to the Right Way*. Pamphlet. Nara: Naikan Kenshujo.

Yoshimoto, Ishin. 1965. *Naikan Yonjū Nen*. Tokyo: Shunshūsha.

————. 1972. Naikan no hoho to jissen. In Okumura, N., et al., eds., *Naikan Therapy*. Tokyo: Igaku Shoin.

————. 1977. *Naikan no Michi*. Nara: Naikan Kenshujo.

————, ed. 1975. *Naikanho*. Nara: Naikan Kenshujo.

————, ed. 1978. *Naidan to Seishin Eisei*. Nara: Naikan Kenshujo.

Index

Index

Lebra, Takie, 103
Love problems, 57–58, 146

Meguro Naikan Center, 62–64, 67–69
Mensetsu interviews, 3, 7–9, 10–11, 15, 18–21, 38, 41, 51, 54, 58, 78, 84, 139–44
Minami Toyota Hospital, 45–46, 62, 67–69
Mizuno, Sensei, 36–37, 51, 80. *See also* Gasshoen Temple
Morita psychotherapy, 2–3, 71, 111–13, 115, 124–26, 143, 147
Mother, vi, 23–24, 28–30, 52, 66, 104, 116, 127–29, 143
Motivation, 64
Mowrer, O.H., 106–10
Murase, Takao, 5, 58, 111

Nagashima, Masahiro, ix, 15, 79
Naikansha, ix, 6, 12–15, 20, 22–27, 31–33, 50, 61–66, 160–61. *See also* Age, Occupation, Residence, Sex ratio
Narita, Toshio, 54
National character, 114
Nichijo Naikan, 2, 22, 25, 146. *See also* Shuchu Naikan

Occupation, 62, 149, 153
Oita Juvenile Detention Facility, 55, 60
Okayama University Naikan, 57
On, 103

Penal institutions, 22, 25, 31, 51–56, 73
Post-Naikan period, 48, 50, 93
Psychoanalysis, 21, 105–6
Psychological tests, 74
Psychotherapy, 30, 49, 53, 71, 87, 97–101, 105–13, 146

Questionnaires, 61–72, 145–46, 160–64

Recidivism, 52, 73, 151. *See also* Penal institutions
Reciprocity, 101–4
Religion, 63, 153. *See also* Shinshu Buddhism, Zen Buddhism

Residence, 154
Rules, 59–60, 115

Sapporo Naikan Zendo, 48–50
Schools, 31. *See also* Delinquency
Selective inattention, 129
Self, 1, 17, 49, 86–87, 90–91, 100, 104, 106, 112, 131–36
Self-protectiveness, 117–21, 136
Senkobo Temple, 40–42, 62–64, 67–70, 82
Sex ratio, 62, 152, 159
Shidosha, ix, 16–20, 67–72, 156–59, 162–64
Shinshu Buddhism, 3, 23, 35, 39–40, 52, 63, 85, 87, 96, 145
Shuchu Naikan, 2, 5, 23. *See also* Nichijo Naikan
Social class, 68, 157
Specification as a therapeutic device, 17, 25–26
Suicide, 75
Symbolic interactionism, 136

Takemoto Ibusuki Hospital, 22, 43–45, 59–60, 62–64, 67–68
Tapes, Naikan, 6, 7, 27, 43, 49, 58, 79, 140
Themes, Naikan, 8, 25, 48
ToDo Institute, 146
Topics, Naikan, 8, 9, 15, 57

Usami, Shue, 40–42, 82. *See also* Senkobo Temple

Values, American, 137–38
Values, Japanese, 115–25
Vocabulary, Naikan, 17

Weekend Naikan, 43, 47
Westerners and Naikan, 70, 73, 127–28, 132, 137–47

Yanagida, Kakusei, 11, 47
Yoga, 48–49

Zadankai, 21–27, 44, 80
Zen Buddhism, 1, 31, 40–42, 48–50, 83, 112, 131